A Diary of
Lettie's Daughter

A Diary of
Lettie's Daughter

MARIAN OLIVIA
HEATH GRIFFIN

Print information available on the last page.

Rev. date: 08/24/2018

To order additional copies of this book, contact:
Xlibris
1-888-795-4274
www.Xlibris.com
Orders@Xlibris.com
782939

CONTENTS

ACKNOWLEDGEMENTS

My mother. Let me acknowledge her with love and gratitude because this diary is about her, her parents, her grandparents, her husband, her children and grandchildren and friends, living and dead.

My siblings. Let me acknowledge my siblings: Phyllis, George, Daniel, Joseph, Nancy and Hattie.

My sister, *Nancy*. I cannot imagine that there are many persons who are more fortunate than I am to have a younger sister as my best friend. When she was born, I was four and a half years old. I knew before I saw her that she would be my very best friend. She is.

Nancy taught me how to be truly accepting and generous to different types of people. She is a special education teacher.

At the time Nancy was born, I was sandwiched between three brothers-one older and two younger. My oldest sibling, Phyllis was the only girl in the family before me. We were destined not to be pals. She taught me how not to treat other people.

George Jr, my oldest brother took good care of me, protected me and defended me when I was little. We tell the story all the time about the day an airplane was flying low (a crop duster) and swooped down near me. I was frightened and started running toward the house where I was born. I was about three years old.

George started running, too and fell on top of me so the plane would not swoop down on me. George, Jr has been my defender and protector all my life and still is. Thank you, big brother.

Daniel and Joseph. Taught me not to be selfish and how to be kind, caring and more giving even when they were selfish. Sometimes they were looking out for *number one*.

Phyllis and Hattie. Taught me how to defend myself from being bullied. They were 'two peas in a pod.' They are now deceased but I miss them.

For this book I am writing, I needed psychological support. I am writing about my mother and father, my siblings and myself. I received much support from George and Nancy. Joe, my youngest brother somehow got squeezed in the bunch. My three other siblings: Phyllis, Daniel and Hattie are deceased.

My eight lovely grandchildren, Nia Olivia, Kiara Janelle, Christian-Paris Bertrand, III, Michael Gerard, II, Amelia Grai Addison, Victoria Olivia, Olivia Christina, and Sophia Morgan – all of you are Griffins.

They are my team. We talk, we bond, they ask questions, they trust me, they are astute as well as loving.

No, I did not skip a generation. My children are so special to me. My four technicians are Bertrand, I, my husband of fifty-five years, Bertrand, II, first son, Keith Phenix, son-in-law and Christian-Paris -first grandson. All I have to do is write. I am thankful that they can e-mail, etc, for me.

Thanks to my researchers who are Michael Gerard, I second son, Karen Michelle, my daughter and Jeanette Shakesnider, my 'proxy' daughter, and Nancy, my sister who travels with me and gathers documents for me.

Let me say thanks to the staff in the East Baton Rouge Parish Library, Scotlandville Branch for guiding and directing me during my research on topics of which I knew nothing, such as Near Death Experience (NDE), Ghosts, out of body experience and 'presence'. They had me reading from morn til night and signing up for the Summer reading program. They include Pamala A. Donaldson, Jennifer L. Thompson and Chad J. Cooper.

To my precious church members at St. Mark United Methodist Church, Baton Rouge, the pastor, Dr. Derrick D. Hills and his wife, Sharron Hills, the ministerial staff, retired Rev. Bertrand Griffin, and retired Rev. Glorious Wright, the musicians, especially Miss Ethel Blaze, (I am a volunteer member of the musician staff), my class leader, Catherine Martin and her husband, Semmie Martin for all their assistance and quality time together over the years, our church secretary, Edna Hickman with her special 'GOOOD MORNING, ST. MARK UNITED METHODIST CHURCH and her giving, caring and expressions of concern and love to all those she meets.

Then there is the Breakfast staff, Dorothy Collins (my little cousin), Michelle Thomas, I taught her a few words in German (Guten Tag), so she wouldn't be so sassy to me, Rosilyn Magee, {a special person to me} and

Ernest Lee, {who is one of our real song birds) whom I see when I walk in the door of the church each Sunday morning, I say thanks for helping me to keep my head together and for your indulgence as you touch other people's lives.

INTRODUCTION

HISTORICAL PERSPECTIVE

The story about my birth and death is begging to be told. It is a story that should not be hidden. My birth happened on the same day, the moment, the minutes that I died. I do remember. These two events happened. I am Lettie's daughter. I have told strangers some of the occurrences of that fateful day, August 29, 1939. I have not told family members.

I choose to write this phenomenon or story as my grandchildren have asked questions. I shall tell my grandchildren that there was 'something to write home about.' I feel comfortable and self- assured with children, especially my eight grandchildren.

Some of the mysteries of life can be the most rewarding experiences of one's life, such as outer body experience and experiencing heaven before you actually die. Very few people have seen a ghost and not been frightened to death by it. Biblical characters have seen angels and been afraid. I have seen both and had an overall calm, serene sense of peace within the realm of the situation.

I feel that I was ushered into heaven to meet my angel and to receive my assignment from God. God truly speaks to us when we need him most. He changes lives, transforms hearts and uses us for good when we are receptive to his will.

I got a glimpse of heaven as an infant. I was introduced to the amazing love of God at the tender age of one day old. Apparently, I accepted the life that God planned for me. I allowed God to speak to me and I heeded his call.

It is not what you think. This could have been a catastrophe occurrence. Many things that happened in our family life were good, comical, blessed and endearing to us as children. We had a wonderful childhood life due to a loving father and a caring mother, thoughtful, wise grandparents (except my paternal grandfather who was hateful and mean.), good, considerate aunts and uncles and great siblings (except Phyllis the oldest sibling who couldn't stand her younger siblings.)

Phyllis must have taken her cantankerousness and contrariness after my paternal grandfather, William 'Will' Heath, Jr. 'Will' Heath had a way with him that would not 'set horses' with anyone except his wife, Hattie (who was our grandmother.) I do not understand how Grandmom Hattie was able to put up with Grandpop 'Will', but she did.

"So we fix our eyes not on what is seen, but on what in unseen. For what is seen is temporary, but what is unseen is eternal. (2 Cor 4: 18 NIV.)

The world stage was on the verge of World War II. Germany was to invade Poland. This was the most devastating event to be happening during my birth date. I ushered in World War II. Or did World War II usher my birth date.

According to African oral tradition, "Every birth is the rebirth of an ancestor." (Follmi, Danielle & Olivier. *Origins-African Wisdom for Every Day*)

"Long before birth, the child as a pre-existing soul, is watched over by a whole line of ancestors down to and including the placenta and the primadian mother that begins to fashion him. (Alassane Ndawe. – Follmi)

Over the years, I have recounted what happened to me as a day-old infant. I've tried to tell the story to other people, only to be disbelieved or shut up.

I am now being brave enough as I swallow my pride to tell a most intimate and blessed story of my life.

When I was eight years old, I tried to tell this story in Sunday school class one day. The minister was sitting in our class that day. He told me not to have that conversation any more because there was no such thing as dying and going to heaven and coming back to life in this day and age, only in biblical times.

He said there was no such thing as being visited by an angel, or seeing ghosts or having out of body experiences (dreams of heaven}.

My father sort of believed me because we had conversations about my birth when I was around two years old. He was the Sunday school superintendent at our church.

When I left class that day, my father told me not to mention my 'dreams' in class any more.

I didn't quite understand what was going on with me, but I knew I was not lying. I did obey both of my parents and kept quiet about my experiences.

I started burying my thoughts and issues deep in my mental diary. These things happened when I was a young child and even during my young adulthood. Yes, I had had an outer body experience, a near death experience, more than once and I have seen ghosts. I buried these things deep.

As I grew up, I was just Marian to my friends and family, not someone who had been visited by my angel. I never thought those around me would believe me or even fathom what I was dealing with.

Both my grandmother Sadie and grandmother Hattie knew about my entrance into this world, that as soon as I was born, I died. They were both mid-wives and were there at the time of my birth.

Mother Lettie died, too.

Was I born to live or born to die. I think that my diary will answer that question. I started writing it the day I was born.

I believe I was put on earth to help out and to save children. I have worked in nurseries at Delaware State University, Atlanta University School of Social Work and Cincinnati, Ohio Social Work agency. I took child psychology and adolescent psychology courses as an undergraduate and graduate student. I have been employed as a case worker in the Aid to Dependent Children in the New Orleans Welfare Department, my first professional job.

I did not want to teach in the conventional way. I did want to teach children to live a better life. I became a social worker and psychological counselor as well as a music teacher and photographer.

I started purchasing dictionaries and thesaurus for the children in my cherubim choir and the other children in our church because our children knew what a computer was, but they had not dealt with a dictionary, a thesaurus and an encyclopedia. Here was the computer age, Ipad, Ipod, Iphone (of which I knew very little} whereby children learn current events and history on these computers.

I organized the cherubim choir at St Mark United Methodist Church in 1975 because there was not a choir for small children. In 2018, forty- six years later, I am still wagging with my cherubim choir and playing the piano for them.

Early in life, I realized my angel in heaven entered my life and brought me back to earth. My mother needed me, my family needed me, others needed me. I did not know who 'others' were. I just ascertained that there was a need and my presence or Holy Spirit urged me on.

Through the years, my mother and I were always close. She knew me and I knew her. There was a communication that I had with my mother, an unspoken word that only she heard. I understood her dependence on me even though I did not always know why she wanted me near her constantly. She felt safe with me and I with her.

Even after I started driving a car at sixteen, I took her everywhere she had to go. Many persons do not have the legacy that we shared. We bonded together all our lives even after she officially died. I was a young adult, twenty years old, in college and a senior when she died.

"Even as adults, few women with mothers want to think about mother loss, still fewer want to hear about it. The loss of a parent as a child is one of the most stressful life-cycle events an individual can face, but without a forum to discuss her feelings, the motherless daughter finds little validation for the magnitude of her loss. Without this recognition the motherless daughter feels like a feminine pariah,(or social outcast), apart and alone." (Edelman, Motherless Daughters.) p. xxiii.

I have no doubt that I have been assigned an angel or several angels who walk with me each day and have been with me all my life. I have dreams, divine interventions, premonitions, fears as well as miracles constantly in my life.

I believe that I have a heavenly mission to fulfill. Some things only God and I know about me. My faith in God was actually given to me at birth. I felt a presence, a constant pressure on me to do something, to act, to motivate, to fight injustice for myself and others.

Even though I became motherless as a young adult, I feel that I have enough endurance, strength and stamina in life to sustain me. All I need is the where-with-all and resources to help sustain me as I am ordained to help mankind. God ordained it.

My eight grandchildren: Nia Olivia, Kiara Janelle, Christian-Paris Bertrand III, Michael Gerard II, Amelia Grai, Victoria Olivia, Olivia Christian, and Sophia Morgan Griffin are always asking me questions. All of them are Griffins. They have a right to know about my life. That is why I am telling my story and my mother's story in the form of a diary.

I believe what my husband, Bertrand Griffin, Sr tells everyone he meets. "You were put here on earth for a purpose. God has a reason for keeping you here."

I have had two heart attacks (according to one of my cardiologist and three surgeries. I have had three defibrillators placed over my heart, over a million dollars worth of surgery because of heart problems.

Bertrand, my husband says, "God is not through with you yet. That is why you are still here."

Bert is a minister/chaplain. He served six years in churches and thirty-six years in the prison ministry as chaplain in one of the largest prisons system in the United States, Angola State Penitentiary.

He also tells everyone he meets that our marriage was made in heaven. We met on a blind date and I was a substitute for the girl he was supposed to meet. I think Bert knows what he is talking about. We have been married fifty- five and a half years.

I recall thinking that I've never doubted that Bert was the man I was supposed to marry. He got upset when I read a letter from another young man that I received as we were sitting in my dormitory in Bumstead hall at Atlanta University.

Bert told me he was not going to sit there a watch me cry over some other man, and I had his engagement ring on my left finger.

"Children, your Grandfather Bert said, 'Marry me next Saturday or give me back my ring."

I answered him by saying, "What time, Bertrand?"

Christian Paris said, "OH snap, Grandpa, You're cool."

"Grandpa Bert planned that wedding. It was beautiful. He contacted the preacher who married us. He told me to get a short white dress, white shoes and a veil. I obeyed."

"Isn't that what you are supposed to do?" asked Karen, our daughter.

The wedding we had on our fiftieth anniversary sufficed after having a very small one that my angel set up for us.

We were students and had no money to get married. However, we did get married with ten student friends as our witnesses.

There were no family members on either side, no mothers, no fathers, no sisters, no brothers. All family members were thousands of miles away in Delaware, Pennsylvania, Virginia, Louisiana and Texas. We married in Atlanta, Georgia.

We were married at 4:00pm. There was another wedding scheduled at that church at 5:00pm. When we finished taking our vows and turned around, the church was full of people.

They had come for our wedding and the 5:00pm wedding. The minister's wife planned a reception for us as a surprise. We did not know most of the people who attended our wedding but they were very gracious to us with many gifts to start our new life together.

The president of Gammon Theological Seminary had an apartment waiting for us within the week. This was the seminary that Bertrand was attending.

"Grandma, you and Grandpa were so lucky. Most people plan their wedding for months and you two got married in a week," said Nia.

I changed graduate schools that semester from Atlanta University because my scholarship was taken from me that spring semester. That spring, I had planned to go back home to Delaware and get a teaching position because I was informed by my dean that she had removed me from the scholarship pool because I had made one C. All my other grades were A's and one B.

My dean, Miss Douglas and I discussed this matter. I felt very vulnerable because I could no longer attend AU without that scholarship. But she said the deed was done. She had given my scholarship to a first year male student and I no longer had my two year scholarship.

After Bert and I got married, I went back to the president of Gammon Theological and asked him for a scholarship. He tole me to fill out an application to attend Gammon and an application for a scholarship. I received both and enrolled in Gammon that semester.

With the blink of an eye, I was back in school, had gotten married to the only man I ever really loved, and we had a new apartment rent free. Life was good.

I told you that I believe the minute I was born, I was sent into heaven to receive my assignment or mission from God. My mother is my earthly angel and my heavenly angel gave me back to her and her to me. Everything after that blessed day was pre -ordained including my marriage to my husband.

I sometimes wonder how other people receive their blessings from God and do not know how they came about.

I read Mary C. Neal's book, 7 *Lessons from Heaven*. She describes that "perhaps because of pride, it took her many years to break through her own *resistance* and begin talking about her near-death experience (NDE) and her blessings."

She said "The truth is, I had been given an assignment in heaven and I was expected to share my story with others and carry out my assignment." p. 2.

She had almost drowned from a Kayak accident. Instead of being frightened and afraid, she felt calm, relaxed and hopeful.

She said, "There are simply no earthly words to describe heavenly wonders." p. 3.

I was steered to another book about Todd Burpo, *Heaven is for Real,* with Lynn Vincent, the author. Just the other day, I read about Todd, a little three and a half year old boy who had a ruptured appendix and needed surgery.

After surgery, Todd's condition worsened. Todd's father, a minister went into one of the hospital chapels and prayed as well as ranted and raved at God.

When his father got enough strength to go back into Todd's hospital room, Todd explained, "I came back, Dad. I came back because you needed me to and God answered your prayer."

Todd told his father that he had died and gone to heaven. "Todd told many tales in spurts."

"There were many children in heaven," Todd said. "They did home work. Jesus was their teacher. Everyone had wings except Jesus. Jesus just went up and down." P. 43.

"Jesus did not need wings, did he, Grandma," said Olivia.

"No," I said. "He was home in heaven."

This book is full of glimpses of what Todd saw in heaven. He did not tell his story about heaven in sequence, just in spurts. He could not have known about the things he said without the intervention of the Trinity: God, Christ and the Holy Spirit.

Todd told his daddy, "The reason I was yelling at you was that Jesus came to get me. He said I had to go back. He was answering your prayer. You needed me to come back to you and mom. I couldn't stay in heaven. Jesus sent me back." p. 47

These stories about God's expectations as well as his graciousness to us is a little better under stood after reading other person's accounts of his caring for us.

"Solomon in Ecclesiastes 3: 1-14 acknowledges the role of God in each season, that our work is a gift of God and that everything God does will endure forever."

Solomon reflects, "there is a time for everything, a time to be born and a time to die, a time to plant and a time to uproot.

Kiara said, "Grandma, I have heard preachers talk like that and I have read that in the Bible."

I said, "My story about my birth and death and heaven has come to me in spurts. I am constantly visited by my angel. I too realize that as an infant, one day old, the Holy spirit visited me that day."

"I am not afraid to die because I have been there. Most of us do not like to think or be reminded of death and be reminded of our mortality. But if we face reality, out of a thousand people alive, a thousand people will die. Yes, all of us will die."

When I had my last surgery, which was last year in February, 2017, I felt calm and happy. I saw many earthly people that I didn't know around me from head to toe. I ask one of the nurses later who all those people were. She told me that a medical student class was there observing my surgery.

I asked for my doctor when I saw so many people around me.

"Do not do anything to me until I see my doctor, Dr. Freddie," I said.

I had faith in God and Dr. Freddie.

The nurse asked someone to find my doctor.

Dr. Freddie entered the operation room and said "Hi."

"I was fine then. I had a calm, safe feeling."

"No, I am not afraid to die, but what I am afraid of is how my loved ones would react to my death and so I do not want to leave them."

"The Lord comes along beside us…" (I Cor: 15 -35).

Much much later, I was expressing what I had been experiencing as a child until now to two elderly ladies in the beauty shop. We were talking and sharing a conversation about seeing our guardian angels, celestial spirits and ghosts.

One of the elderly ladies said more or less what Dan Walsh said in his book, *What Follows After*.

"The young look forward, the old look back." P. 7.

Funny how the memory works. You can think you forgot something like its gone for good. Then you hear a song from fifty years ago, and it unlocks a door. One you haven't opened for so long you forgot it was even there. It triggers a replay of one of the worst or best moments of your life.(Walsh, p. 16.)

Miss Patsy in the beauty shop said to me, "Conquer your fears, and capture your dark memories. Don't tell anyone else your stories. Go right home and write them down. That way, the whole world can read them."

That was my que. I went home and prayed about it. The Old Testament gave me encouragement though I Samuel 7:8. When I read how Samuel interceded for God's people as they faced trouble, I was strengthened to pray for myself and the people I love. (I Samuel 7:7 NIV).

I prayed: "Dear Lord, the way you answer my prayers amazes me. Strengthen my faith and trust in you."

Here it is: A Diary of Lettie's Daughter.

CHAPTER I

MY MOTHER LETTIE

My dear Grandchildren:

This is Mother's Day, May 13, 2018. I am so happy to see each of you. The eight of you are so precious to me. Nia Olivia, Kiara Janelle, Christian-Paris, Michael Gerard, II, Amelia Grai, Victoria Olivia, Olivia Christina and Sophia Morgan. All of you are Griffins and you are here with me.

"Granny, you told me one time that everyone has a story to tell," said Christian-Paris.

"Tell us a story about yourself this time. You have never told us anything about yourself, Grandma," Victoria said.

"I want to play cards. Grandma, do you still have UNO cards?" asked Amelia Grai.

"Yes I do. Let me go get them."

"Lil Mike and Christian-Paris, set up the card table and we will go from there," I told my lovely grandchildren."

"Yea' said Victoria. 'We made mothers' day cards for you to tell you what we want to say to you."

But we still want you to tell us a story," my little nine year old Victoria 'story bandit' said.

"We want a story, we want a story," chimed Olivia and Sophia together.

"Let us all settle in the den," I said.

Our den is a real family room. We have two lime green sofas sitting on two large multi-colored pink and green rugs, (of course, I am an Alpha Kappa Alpha Sorority member) two glass coffee tables with ornaments from Africa and Asia, candy dishes and fruit bowls on them. Two lamps on lamp tables are beside the sofas.

Now Grandpa Bert has his old rocking chair that his mother gave to us over fifty years ago when we first moved to Baton Rouge. Whenever we have company, Grandpa Bert claims his rocking chair.

The large fire place is on the back wall which adequately heats the den. We don't need the fire place today. It's springtime.

Sophia left the spacious den where the Griffin family had all gathered on Willow Springs Avenue. Her favorite place to play in our house is the play room. We have dolls and doll houses, play kitchens, trains and cars, balls and pianos in the play room. The same types of toys are at their house in New Orleans. However, Sophia wanted someone to play with her in the play room.

After eating a sumptuous dinner, the adults wanted to relax or take a nap.

Sophia ran back into the room and threw a small rubber doll on the floor. She stood and laughed. He mother, Tracie picked her up and placed Sophia on her lap. 'SoSo'(her nickname) is our youngest grandchild. She had turned four years old in April and she has lots of energy.

She was satisfied in her mother's lap and leaned back against her mother and settled down. Sophia had eaten very little food but needed lots of attention from the adults in the room. Her mother understood that.

The adults and other children had eaten to their hearts content. The food was delicious.

Michael, Sr had brought his famous gumbo and rice which he is so proud of. It was as if he had caught the crabs and shrimp himself. There is no humbleness about Michael when it came to his gumbo. He always told people that his aunt Darcus taught him how to make seafood gumbo and cherry delight, a special type of pie.

I'll admit that I never learned how to make the cherry delight pie, but I thought I had showed Michael how to make the rue for the gumbo. After the rue which is the gravy that thickens the gumbo, everything else in simple. Just add seasoning, chicken, sausage and seafood, and voila! There's gumbo in the big pot.

Tracie had fixed boudin balls and macaroni and cheese which she and the little ones love. Now boudin and boudin balls is something I have never tried to make, but I love to eat them.

Karen's specialty is always potatoes and sausage. I have been trying her recipe. I haven't quite mastered it yet.

Keith, Karen's husband, brought a pound cake, and a nut, raisins and carrot cake. He is a cake purest. Don't bring any cakes around him because he will insult you.

Bertrand, II and Kotosha brought sweet potato and pecan pies. They find the best pies wherever they can drop their money. Tony's Seaford store is the best place for pies and I might even pick up the pies for them. Kotosha is going to pay me for them anyway.

Grandpa Bert makes a great cornbread even thought it does come out of a box. You have to have the right ingredients to make it taste special. OH, and Bert always provides the ice cream.

I make all the vegetables: cabbage, collard greens, yellow squash with pure butter and hamburger meat, candied yams and mashed potatoes, pasta and rice for backup.

Great grandmother, Lear Chase, our grandchildren's great grandmother, sent fried alligator and stewed okra. She owns the Dookie Chase famous restaurant in New Orleans.

Our nieces, Francine, Linda, Whitney and Aggie brought the drinks and other junk food to nibble on after dinner. They live in another town about thirty miles away but they come for all special occasions.

This year we invited several church families over. Ms. Mandy Avila brought a large pineapple upside down cake and some brownies. The Carson family of five children and their mother brought good appetites.

"OH, Grandma," said Victoria.

The two church families left early to make the rounds for dinner as they had more invitations to honor.

Amelia Grai had the UNO cards in her hand trying to shuffle them.

"I'm going to win," she said.

Her older brother, Michael, II whom I call 'Lil Mike' said with a smirk,

"Here, give me the cards. Let me shuffle them. We can still hear Grandma tell her story. I believe she is trying to get out of telling us about herself."

"OK, Lil Mike, I'll tell you the short version of a long story. It's a whopper," I said.

"What do you mean, it's a whopper?' said seven year Olivia?"

"By that, I mean you have to put on your 'faith cap' to believe this one."

Karen, Keith and Christian-Paris had arrived on Friday night and we spent Saturday cooking and cleaning up. They were tired. I was tired.

Nia and Kiara had gone out of the room to change clothes and get comfortable after a good church service at St Mark.

. They had flown in from Atlanta the night before and had gotten up early to attend church with us on Mother's day. They returned to the den as all the family was returning to their comfort zones.

"OK, Grandma!" Nia pointed out. 'Your stories are beginning to be horrific."

Eleven year old Amelia _Grai, becoming interested, said "what's that, Nia?"

"I mean Grandma is about to tell us a story that might be scary,"

"Well we are all together and I'm going to tell you a personal experience that I have not told other family members yet."

Grandpa Bert said, "OH Gush. I'm about to hear something that I have never heard from your grandmother. I am all ears."

Grandpa Bert is very tolerant with me and the grandchildren. Sometimes he finds another spot in the house from whichever one we are in and pulls out his favorite book. He has always been an avid reader since I've known him. We respect that and try to talk and play quietly.

Wow, we are favored with his presence today. I guess that is because it is mother's day and there are several mothers in the house.

"Grandpa Bert, this story is PG-13. I don't know if your ears should hear this," I said jokingly to Bert."

"Bring it on Grandma, my ears are old enough to hear anything even though I am hard of hearing. You know you can tell me anything," Grandpa Bert mused. He stood up and kissed me.

The children and grandchildren laughed.

CHAPTER II

MY BIRTH

"I call this story a diary written by me when I was born up to the present time. Actually it began the day I was born. It was August 29, 1939. My mother was having serious complications around the time of my birth. She was having a breathing problem among other painful physical and psychological episodes that go with childbirth."

It's amazing how much an individual experiences, learns, remembers and comprehends as an infant or small child. It is even more amazing what one actualizes and perceives about oneself, how much one remembers when we become elderly and old as I consider myself.

My birth was becoming a serious problem or obstacle for Mother. "Life is a process of breaking through challenges and impediments."

Ryan Holiday in his book, *The Obstacle is the Way,* indicates that every obstacle is unique to each of us. But the responses they elicit are the same: fear, frustration, confusion, helplessness and depression." p. 1.

"OH, Grandma, there you go again with those big words. You got to talk to us like we are little children," Quips Amelia Grai.

"OK, smart mouth, I'll try to break it down for you," I said.

"Naturally I did not know anything about my mother's childbearing episodes with the first four children born to my parents. Two siblings lived, Phyllis, then George.

Two twin boys died. How was I to know that the burden of stillborn infants was to weigh so heavily on my mother and father psychologically, physically, spiritually, mentally and emotionally. Their whole being was involved, Daddy as well as Mother.

This unfortunate, helpless, situation created frustration in the family in which there was no way out. How to have more children while losing them or not having children when there was no method to avoid having them. That's what was happening. The family could not come out of some their situations unscathed.

"Grandma," Said Victoria, "You use such big words. Sometimes I don't know what you are talking about."

"Victoria, there's a song that the old folk used to sing. 'We'll understand it better bye and bye. Just live and learn. One day you will understand."

"I did not always know what my grandparents were talking about either. But I do now. I learned much that has helped me on my way in later life." Let me get on with the punch lines of my story or you will never hear the end of it," I said.

"Meanwhile, let me just say, when I was born, we were poor. There were outside episodes going on that a small child would not understand.

Daddy was trying to earn money with whatever skills he had. He was painting this tiny wooden doll house and a model airplane the day before I was born. Mother did not let him know that the fumes were upsetting her stomach. She had a terrible headache and was nauseated. Your great great Grandmom Sadie, came by each and every day to check on my Mother.

Anyway, the next day I was born. Then I died. My mother was very sick. She died. My daddy walked a mile to get Grandmom Sadie, my mother's mother. He had no choice. We had no telephone, no cell phone, no text, no Ipad, no car. And we were poor. So we had no doctor.

Besides we were black and no doctor was going to come to a black family's house to deliver a baby. Grandmom Sadie was a mid -wife.

The family was in turmoil.

Holiday says it best, "turning trials into triumph is the way." He has a way of expressing "What stands in the way becomes the way. Each and every obstacle should be turned into an opportunity to practice some virtue: patience, courage, humility, resourcefulness, reason, justice and creativity. (p. xv.)

Amelia Grai said, "Grandma, you are scaring me. I do not really know what turmoil is and I'm scared of having babies."

"Amelia Grai, God has it under control. He sends help when we need it. And we need Him at all times. Only He can make a human life. We just have to trust what He does.

"Well, would you know it. My other Grandmother was a mid-wife also. Daddy sent his brother, Leon to bring their mother, Grandmom Hattie to our little cabin.

Leon lived in Philadelphia and would drive through Seaford, Delaware to see Daddy and his family on his way to Virginia to see their mother Hattie. It was God- sent that Leon came that day before I was born and was able to bring Grandmom Hattie back with him. They were expecting Grandmom Hattie at any time.

My mother and father and my two older siblings, Phyllis and George, Jr lived in a small cabin behind Mr. Smyth' big colonial style home. Down south we call them plantations. Daddy worked for Mr. Smyth so he got to live in one of his shacks (I mean cabin.)

"Grandma, you're something else," said Kiara. "You are very funny. You mean just what you say, don't you."

"Well, I tell it like it is. My birth was a doozy." We were poor. Daddy was the only one working. He worked on the farm for Mr. Smyth, then he had gotten a job helping to build a road in our small town. He worked up into the night trying to get his work done every day and make ends meet.

He was also building model airplanes and doll houses and displaying them to make extra money every year at the Delaware State Fair.

Mother and Daddy had used Mother's money that she had saved from playing the piano and giving piano lessons. She gave the money to Daddy so that he could buy a piece of land in Greenwood.

"Let that be a lesson to you," I said.

"What, Grandma?" asked Lil Mike.

"Saving your money so that you can buy the bigger things that you want or need, not just frivolous little things like candy all the time," I said

Nia stated indignantly, "Grandma, I thought you were going to tell the short version of your story. Can you get to the point."

"Patience, Nia. Patience. The old folk and the babies want to hear the longer version of my diary." I know you have other things to do. You are in college and talking on the phone with your friends is pretty important to you, too."

Nia said, "When I go back to college, I have to take my finals for this semester. I need to study."

"Go ahead, Nia. Go study,' I said.

"Now Grandma, You know you got me interested. Let's hear the diary story."

Well, the day I was born, Daddy went to get my grandmother who lived about a mile away through the woods. Grandmom Sadie arrived from the Fountain homestead with Daddy in a few minutes. I was being born. Here I am. One minute. I knew my mother. My mother knew me. Then all was gone. I died. Mother died.

I looked at my grandchildren. They were very still. I decided to continue.

"The small bed room in our cabin was hot and steamy and dark."

"There is no formidable way to have a baby but to have a baby"

. My two grandmothers used to say "you go down in the valley" when you are having a baby.

TWO GRANDMOTHERS – MID-WIVES

My two grandmothers were in this small bedroom working over Mother and me. This was my parent's bedroom. My older siblings, Phyllis and George slept in another room on pallets. Grandmom Sadie later walked back home to her own house to rest and sleep. She lived within walking distance from our little cabin.

Grandmom Hattie had to stay overnight because she lived in Virginia and could not come and go as Grandmom Sadie did. Grandmom Hattie slept in the room with Phyllis and George.

Olivia Christina came to a conclusion with "Grandma, if you died when you were born, how come you are living now?."

"I think my diary will answer that question. I started writing it the day I was born. You see, my angel came to me and started singing."

"What did she sing, Grandma?" asked Olivia.

I reported, "She sang, 'Jesus loves me' and 'We shall overcome.'"

"We sing those songs, Grandma. How did you know them and you were just a baby?"

My angel knew I needed her and came to me. The two of us were up high over my mother and me and my two grandmothers. Grandmom Sadie was holding me and Grandmom Hattie was on her knees praying.

She was not alone. Jesus was on her left with his hand on her left shoulder. He was praying, too. Another man was on his knees praying. He had his hand on my Grandmom Hattie's right shoulder. He was praying. This man was

Richard Allen." Grandmom Hattie was holding Mother's hand. They were all touching.

"Grandma, you are brilliant. How did you know who Jesus was and how did you know Richard Allen when you were born?' said Victoria

"I never heard of Richard Allen. I have heard of Jesus," she said.

"Victoria, after I had a dispute with my Sunday school teacher and Daddy one Sunday morning in church about my seeing Richard Allen as a baby, I went to the school encyclopedia, The New Encyclopedia Britannica, and found him.

"Richard Allen was born in Philadelphia on February 14, 1760 and died March 26, 1831. He was the founder and first bishop of the African Methodist Episcopal Church, a major U.S. denomination."

"I will tell you more about him later," I said.

Grandpa Bert was sitting in the rocking chair with his head down. He knew that I always played with the grand kids and loved to tell them stories and feed them.

He sat straight up on that one.

He said, "I need to hear this story myself. You have told me many things about your childhood in the past fifty-five years we've married but you never told me that you had died and an angel saved you, Marian."

"And you never told me that you had seen Richard Allen as an infant." He was shocked.

I wondered if he was going to object to my telling our grandchildren this story. It was a doozy.

Lil Mike, Amelia Grai and Christian-Paris had dealt the cards and were arguing over the rules of the game as usual. First hand, you play cards this way, second hand of cards, you play cards that way. On and on and on.

Christian-Paris said, "I play, I win. No if ands and buts about it," he promised.

"Nada," said Amelia. I'm listening to this story." She threw her cards back into the deck.

"*A Diary of Lettie's Daughter's* is what I named this story,"

"A diary of Lettie's daughter?"

"Grandma, that is a strange name for a story." Amelia Grai quipped.

"I know, but it just came to me. I have been writing this story in my brain for a long, long time. But I just named it.

"You will see. It is about my mother, my father, my siblings and me, and all of you."

"My angel told me the day I was born that I had twin brothers who had died the year before I was born. They were in heaven. They were lost to my mother and father, but they were not lost to Jesus," I said.

"When I was almost two years old, my mother picked me up and carried me outside to her garden at our new house that Daddy was building. The house was not finished but Daddy had moved us into it because Mr. Smyth was angry with him for building his own house."

Mother's garden was very precious to her and later I understood why. She could pray and think and hope in her garden.

Marjorie Holmes said it best in her book, I've Got to Talk to Someone, God.

> This is my garden, God, this is my garden, my own small precious portion of the earth that you have made. I will dig and hoe and tend it. I will grub in the soil that is cool and moist and scented with spring.
>
> I will find you in that soil as I crumble its clods or press these small seeds deep into the dark flesh. What a joyful thing, the feel of your silent soil. It clings to my fingers, it is hard and certain beneath my knees.
>
> It receives my little offerings – these tine plants these slips and cuttings, these infinitesimal seedlings, with a kind of blind, uncommenting magnificence. I am a trifle awed before it, I am filled with an amused humility.
>
> How insignificant I am that I should be entrusted with this miracle to come. No, no the earth will surely reject my anxious efforts, my foolish hopes. Yet I know a happy patience too.
>
> Wait, only wait upon the Lord, as the Bible says.
>
> And sure enough. The silent, teeming forces of certain creation set to work and soon the miracle has come. p.118.

Mother had a special infinity for her gardens.

Daddy was still working for Mr. Smyth but no longer lived in the old shack (cabin) behind the big beautiful colonial home with spacious lawns and trees and shrubbery. Daddy never did let Mother work in the big house. Mother was educated.

"I got that," said Christian-Paris. "I feel my great grandpa's pain. He was awesome."

There were two other older women that worked in the big house. One was the washwoman and other was the cook and housekeeper. The details about the house setup were told to me much later by my father. It required stamina and grit to work in the big house because you were treated like dirt. Daddy didn't want that treatment for my mother. It's another whole story.

Anyway, Mother had started her own garden at our own house in Greenwood. She liked to hoe in her garden early in the morning after she sent my older sister and brother to school.

"It is cool and calm," she said, "no one to bother her."

She always gave me a bottle so I could nibble on the nipple.

She told me later in life, "You were a good baby, very seldom cried or fussed."

This morning when we went outside, Mother was crying. She sat me down on the soft grass and picked up her hoe. Then she stood just looking into space.

"Don't cry, mother," I said.

"My twin brothers are in heaven." She sat down on the grass beside me.

"Tell me again what you just said," my mother wanted to know.

"I saw my twin brothers the day I was born. They came and kissed me.

"Mother needs you," they said. "Go back to her."

"That day, I woke up. I was lying on my mother's breast. She was kissing my forehead and crying. I put my hand to my mother's face and she stopped crying."

Grandmom Sadie picked me up again and held me. Grandmom Hattie attended to my mother. Daddy came into the room. He was crying.

"In my whole life, that is the only time I ever saw my father cry," I said.

Daddy knew Mother was sick and he walked the floor all night. She had been sick for several days. Grandma Sadie rode her old grey mare to our little cabin each day to see Mother. Mother had told her she believed the baby would come early. Mother was regurgitating all day.

"Really, Grandma, an old grey mare," said Kiara. She started laughing.

I was glad the children were picking up the lighter side of the story. I did not want to frighten them. But I felt they had a right to know. They had asked for the story.

"As I said before, Daddy was painting a little model airplane and doll house and the fumes were getting to Mother. He had won first place at the state fair of Delaware the year before for his models and was trying to win first place this year. The prize was three dollars.

"Three dollars!" exclaimed Lil Mike. "That is no prize money at all."

"Lil Mike, three dollars for a black man to win at a state fair in 1939 was very special. All the other person's objects in that category were not as well built enough to even be placed on display. The judges decided to be fair with Daddy and give him the prize money both years."

Daddy was building the house we lived in all my childhood days," I said.

Fifteen year old Lil Mike said, "Dad Built our house, the one we live in now. And I remember when he built our house in Birmingham. Man! That was something!"

"You liked that house?" said Big Mike.

Tracie chimed in," I especially liked the location and our neighbors. We also moved in while Michael was still building our house. And we had plenty of company all the time. We were the only part of the family who lived in Birmingham, Alabama.

"So, the rest of our whole family lived in Louisiana. My parent and grandparents and aunts and uncles all lived in New Orleans. Michael's parents live in Baton Rouge."

"They had somewhere to come when we lived in downtown Birmingham and they came for every occasion: birthdays, mother's day, father's day, Christmas, you name it," said Big Mike.

"Wow, don't forget hurricane Katrina's fall on New Orleans. All the Haydels and Chases came to Birmingham for over a month. Thank God we made room for them at our house and friends' houses," said Big Mike.

"Yes, those were turbulent times. Yet God sustained us all," Grandpa Bert said.

"I am reminded of Joshua when he was about to die. He shared a message to the Israelites that recounted all God had done for them."

He noted, "You lived in the wilderness for a long time. God gave you a land on which you did not toil and cities you did not build; and you lived in them and ate from the vineyard and olive groves that you did not plant.

Joshua set up a large stone to remind the people of Israel of God's provision." Joshua 24: 7-26 NIV.

"Yea, I liked that house," Lil Mike continued.

"It was right up town with the big boys. We had all kinds of good stuff up town in Birmingham. We would go to the zoo and the black museum and the church that got bombed in Birmingham. Man! That was something!"

"Lil Mike, your daddy is pretty much like my daddy, who is Big Mike's grandfather. My daddy, George Heath was a builder: houses, a restaurant, a grocery store, other buildings, roads and bridges. He really knew how to mix and pour concrete.

He did not have a college degree but he was brilliant, an engineer." His parents Hattie and William 'Will' Heath, Jr were builders, also. They built their own house and store in Virginia."

"Your father, Michael Griffin I, has many of his grandfather and great grandparents' traits and skills. Big Mike has built two houses for your family and continues to built clinics for the company he works for and that is no easy task."

"Lil Mike, you too are a builder. It's in your blood. Your mother's side of the family are builders and developers: houses and a restaurant as well. You love building blocks and lego. You are talented and fortunate."

"I heard you say the other day that you want to be an engineer. I say 'yes' to that. You come from a long line of builders," I said.

I loved the house in Birmingham that you lived in and your parents took us to so many of those historical places when we came to your birthday parties and other occasions," I said.

"Grandma, you forgot all about the day you were born and all that malarkey," said Nia.

"Grandma, you are getting off the subject," said Christian-Paris.

"I tend to do that when the subject is getting heavy. I am afraid that you will not understand what I am saying, so I try to cut it short. Remember, I said I would give you the short version of my story and this story can never be told in a straight line. Life is just not like that."

"We want the long version," said Victoria. "What happened after great grand daddy won the fair money? When Grandmom Sadie came out of the bedroom into the kitchen?"

Well, Daddy came home with the prize money and showed it to my mother the day before I was born. She was pleased and told him to put in on the little night stand under the scarf.

Grandmom Sadie was very worried. She told my Daddy, "Send for your mother. We will need her."

Daddy told Grandmom Sadie that he had asked his brother Leon to bring their mother back with him from Virginia.

The day before I was born, Uncle Leon, Daddy's brother had come to our cabin. Then the next morning he brought Grandmom Hattie back with him. She was God sent.

Grandmom Sadie was so nervous. This was her only daughter. She hated to see her suffer like this.

"Grandma, how do you know all of this?" asked Kiara.' You never go in a straight line when you tell us stories."

"I was there," I said. "My angel and I were there together."

My Angel and I

"I cannot tell a story about my family in a straight line. There are so many twists and turns in my family as I said before. Suffice it to say that when I began oral history or tradition, I am speaking from my mind and imagination as well as any God- given talent that I might have."

"When I was two, I was sitting on the grass with my mother. She had a faraway look in her eyes. I knew she was troubled. She was crying."

I said, "Don't worry, Mother. My brothers are alright. They are in heaven."

Mother was stunned.

"Now you know right where they are. They are together in heaven with Jesus," I told my mother.

"Mother said, "you are so little, yet you know so much. Only your father and I and my mother knew that I lost a baby last year after two months of-----""

"Mother, it was two boys," I cut her off.

"I tell you. I was with them and my angel and Jesus. They did tell me I needed to go back. They just kissed me. Then I opened my eyes and you were kissing me, Mother. That's when I knew you."

"I always have my angel with me," I told Mother." You are going to have two more boys and you are going to name them Daniel and Joseph because you love those two men in your Bible that you keep under your pillow."

"How do you know that I keep my Bible under my pillow? It is very sacred to me and I don't want anyone touching my Bible," she said.

"I know, Mother. I see you reading it when I'm sleeping on your bed." My two year old little 'know it all self' said.

When Daddy came in from work that evening, Mother told him about our conversation that we had in the garden that morning.

Daddy said, "Thank God." Now we will get some relief from losing our baby".

Mother said, "George, Marian said it was two babies. We didn't know that. We did not know they were boys. We were going to name our baby *Marian* last year after my friend from childhood."

She was referring to Marian Anderson. Mother and Marian Anderson were both born in Philadelphia in the adjourning or same neighborhood. Mother was born on December 6, 1908. Marian Anderson was born on February 27, 1902. (There is some discrepancy about the birth date of Marian Anderson which bears further research.)

"We did not know we had twin boys. It's hard to swallow, but I believe Marian. She knows so much about the sequence of occurrences and events, it is hard not to believe her. She has a certain tranquility about her story and she tells everything in sequence. There is no false perception about what she says. Besides Marian is too little to know how to make up things."

"Oh my God. What's going to become of this child. She has a gift but it could also be a curse. She has a uniqueness not readily understood or accepted by others. We will have to watch her very closely."

Mother and Daddy did not know that I could hear them. I was in my bed in the 'girls' room. They were in their bed room.

"Marian has a determination that I did not see in the two older children. It's like she is grown or has been here before. She is going to meet many challenges but she is going to meet them head on. She is going to be equal to the task. She will be connected to others."

"She will be well loved and well hated. No matter what circumstances are put upon her, she will accept it and deal with it," My Mother stated.

Daddy said, "How do you know this much about this infant child?"

Mother said, "She's quite a bit like me. She will love hard like I do. She will be hurt often and struggle much but she will overcome great obstacles. That will be her way out of situations. Marian already has a good head on her shoulder."

CHAPTER III

MY GHOSTS

Olivia said, "Grandma, have you ever seen a ghost?"

"Yes, I've seen my mother three times since her actual death. The first time was about six or eight months after she died in January, 1961. I was in graduate school in the Atlanta University School of Social Work in Georgia.

I was sitting in one of my classmate's dormitory room. There were several female students in the room. It was Saturday afternoon. Betty had just received a package from her parents. There were lots of goodies in the box. Betty was examining the contents of the box. The other girls were going "Oh and Ah" over all the food.

Betty turned to me and said, "Marian, you gets none of this food 'cause you don't ever have anything to share."

"I jumped up and ran out of the room. I was truly hurt. I thought Betty and Beverly were my best friends at Atlanta University. We took all our classes together at the School of Social Work and we would go to the library every night to study and do our paper work," I said.

"I went into my room down the hall and fell on my bed. I was half way asleep when I was awakened by a shadow passing over my face."

I sat up and hollowed, "Mother." She moved over me, turned her back and moved swiftly away."

I jumped up and ran back to Betty's room.

When I flung open the door, Betty said, "Marian, you look like you've seen a ghost."

"I did. My Mother," I said.

Betty said, "You told me your mother was dead. I know you told us your mother died last year."

"She is dead but I just saw her," I said. "She was a ghost. I was so hurt when I left your room. I was thinking "what good am I to anyone. I don't have anything to give or share, and I......"

Betty ran to me and hugged me.

"I'm so sorry I said those mean things to you, Marian. You are my best friend and I love you."

"We were all in the room crying. It was about five overgrown twenty-one year old babies in the room crying."

Then we started making tuna fish salad and crackers and cheese cake. We had a good time. All our woes were forgotten.

"When I think about that moment, that day, I realize that Mother was pushing my back out into the playing field.

'Don't feel sorry for yourself, do something about your situation," she was saying to me.

"Don't ever feel sorry for yourself. Remember what I taught you."

"You are a child of God."

"You are too mixed up to hate anybody. Your blood is mixed with everyone on earth."

"Do not let anyone else rule your mind. You are strong and resilient."

"Love yourself and love everybody."

"Go away and make your own way. Stand on your own two feet."

Mother reminded me of all these things she had taught me in one split second.

"As I am writing this," I said, "I am crying." Every year after that first year Mother died in January 30, 1961, I would wake up crying. I would run in the bathroom so that Grandpa Bert would not see me.

The year after Bertrand II was born, I woke up crying and couldn't stop. I had to go to work that morning. Grandpa Bert heard me crying and came into the bathroom and ask me what was the matter.

I replied, "My mother died and now she will never get to see our baby."

"What are you talking about? Your mother has been dead for several years. I didn't even get to meet her," said Grandpa Bert.

"Seems like it was yesterday," I said. "She hits my imagination every year around this time. It's just that sometimes it's worse."

Hope Edelman in her book, *Motherless Daughters*, describes the situation: "Mothers don't die young. Mothers are immortal. Mothers don't die and leave the children they love."

I was called from the hospital by my Uncle Clarence the day Mother died. "Lettie died," he said.

It was Monday evening around four o'clock on January 30, 1961. I was called to the hall telephone in my dormitory at Delaware State University. I was a senior getting ready to graduate in May, '61."

Even though Mother had been ill for quite a while and in the hospital for two months, I couldn't believe Mother was dead.

As I read Edelman's book, I understood what one person said: "Kristen still speaks of the lost of her mother with incredulity."

She said, 'If you'd asked me years ago if I thought my mother could die, I would have said, 'No way. I'd never, ever thought about it. I knew no one in my secluded, little town whose mother had died. I thought it couldn't happen to me because my family was so happy. My mother's death completely rocked my world."

"Kristen expressed it best for me. Sickness was one thing, death was totally different. I couldn't imagine someone that close to me dying," I said.

"Mother and I had a special relationship that deserves special articulation lacking words to express how I still feel. Of all the relationships that I had in my childhood as well as my adulthood, my mother had the most profound and deepest effect on me, on my life. She just taught us so many things that turned out to be the truth."

My mother said, "You are no better or no worse than anyone else. You are too mixed up to hate anyone."

"What does that mean, Grandma?" Said Kiara.

"It means love thy neighbor as thyself. Who is thy neighbor? Anyone you meet. Persons seen and unseen. All the world is a stage, all belongs to God. We all belong to him."

Shay Rieser stated in her book, *Our Family*, "that one of her family members believed that all people belong to a world family. As in personal families, there are many differences, but it is just these differences that add to the value and joy of life." p. 1.

"That year she died, I missed my mother so much. I was far from home in Atlanta. I had left two younger sisters, Nancy and Hattie at home in Delaware.

Daddy was grieving but he had moved on away from the family. My two little sisters had to fend for themselves. Our three brothers, George, Daniel and Joseph were all in the navy. We did not know where Phyllis, our oldest sister was," I said.

"Focusing exclusively on what is in our power magnifies and enhances our power. To see an obstacle as a challenge, to make the best of it, is always a choice. Every ounce of energy directed at things we can't actually influence is wasted. That is self- indulgence and self- destructive."(Holiday, p. 44.)

"Children, I'll tell you about my other ghost stories later, some of them are too painful." I said.

Olivia said, "Grandma, I started this. I want to hear more about your ghosts. I think I've seen one.

Victoria said, "Olivia, you haven't seen no ghost."

Olivia Christina snapped back, "Leave me alone, 'Toria'. "I have seen a ghost. I was dreaming about a little baby boy one night. When I woke up and sat up, he smiled at me then he went away. Now I want to hear about Grandma's ghost."

She repeated, "I want to hear about Grandma's ghost."

"Well, Olivia and Victoria," I said, "my second sighting of a ghost was when I went back to my other graduate school in 1973. I had received my second masters degree in psychological counseling from this seminary in May 1965.

Your grandpa Bert went to this school, New Orleans Baptist Theological Seminary to receive training in chaplaincy and crisis counseling. The closest seminary to us where we lived in Baton Rouge was in New Orleans at the Baptist Seminary.

"Grandpa Bert started his training at Baptist Hospital of New Orleans. One night a week, Grandpa Bert had to do a twenty-four hour shift, he was gone all day."

"Around mid-night the night of his first all night shift, I stirred because I heard one of the children moaning. As I raised up to go see about the children (I did not know which child it was, Bertrand, II, Karen or Michael), a white form flew over my head.

I hollered 'Nano'. (That was my mother-in-law's nick name.) She moved back over me and turned around and flew away. I just sat there and started praying. I knew my mother- in – law was ill and we were very concerned about her."

When Grandpa Bert came home that next morning, he went straight to bed. I got up and prepared breakfast for the children because they went to nursery school each day. By the time we left, Grandpa Bert was fast asleep.

I was taking two classes each day at the seminary. This particular day I was perturbed. I did not know how to approach the subject of having seen Nano (Bert's mother) in the form of a ghost. Nano, my mother- in- law and I were close. We shared secrets.

Later I found out that she did not always tell her three children some of the things that she told me because she did not want to disturb them about some things she had experienced when she was younger.

Anyway, that evening the family returned to the apartment on the seminary campus after classes for me. hospital work for Grandpa Bert and nursery school for the three children: Bertrand II, Karen Michelle and Michael Gerard.

Grandpa Bert was sitting on the sofa. He got up and kissed me. Then he kissed all three of the children.

"My mother is so sick" he said. "I might have to go to Alexandria to see about her."

She was in the hospital. Darcus, Bert's sister, had just called Bert. It was Friday afternoon.

I thought that it was strange that Bert said 'go see *about* her, not go see her.'

I said, "let's go." I started packing the three children's clothes from their closet. When I came into our bedroom, I pulled out my one white dress."

"Be sure to pack your Black suit and tie," I said. Bert looked at me strangely.

"That's the only way that I could tell him I had seen his mother in a death mode. We rode from New Orleans to Baton Rouge. We lived in Baton Rouge. We stopped at our home. Bert did not say one word to me. He went into the house. Our children were asleep so I stayed in the car. Bert stayed so long, I went in to get him. He was just sitting in the bathroom. I took his hand and said, "Let's go, again."

The two of us locked up our house in Baton Rouge and got back into the car and started on to Alexandria, Louisiana. I kept looking at him. Finally I said," let me drive." He had his eyes closed, or so near closed I could not see them open.

Grandpa Bert drove straight to the hospital. He went into the hospital. Nano had just died.

We woke the children up and walked in the hospital and on into the family waiting room. My sister-in-law Darcus came into the waiting room and stood there crying. She took Bert's hand and walked out the waiting room crying.

They were both crying. They needed a moment to themselves with their mother.

"OH, Grandma, That's so sad," said Nia, our first grandchild. "When my other Grandpa Redmond died, the preacher said, "Dying is a part of life. I guess I understand it better now. I believe my Nano is in heaven."

"I believe Nano looked up and saw Heaven. She got a glimpse of heaven and came back to visit us in the form of a ghost to say goodbye. She was a good person," I said to my grandchildren.

Grandpa Bert looked up and said," Anybody for ice cream and pie. We need a break."

"I'll say *Amen* to that," said Bertrand, ll, both about the heaven scene and the mention of ice cream and pie.

Recently I read a library book by Todd Burpo with Lynn Vincent. This book was called *Heaven is for Real*. This book revealed that a young three year old boy told his parents that he was visited by an angel when he was in the hospital having his appendix removed. The appendix had burst and Todd was in serious condition. He was visited by an angel from heaven who told him about a sister who died in child birth. When he told his mother and father that he knew about his deceased sister, they were amazed because they had not told Todd about a sister.(Vincent, P.20).

I know that some of us get warnings, or premonitions or a fresh point of view to prepare us for what is to come. I use to get warnings or see visions of something that was going to happen and just start praying.

"From the time I was seven years old to the time I was a young adult, I would envision that my whole family was going to get killed. I prayed all night many times that the Lord would keep my family safe. After praying hard, I was reminded that we were safe. God was watching over us. We had angels walking with us. I believed that," I said.

"Marian is going to be the salvation of us all, just you wait and see," Daddy used to utter these words to me all the time.

It seemed as if he were talking to me, and yet someone else. He always talked at me in the third person but he was addressing me.

"I wondered what he meant but I tried to be good all the time while my siblings were always getting into trouble. If we did something wrong through the week, Daddy would whip us on that Friday night. I was scared of a whipping, especially by Daddy. He whipped hard."

The Whippings

Grandpa Bert told the children, "your grandmother related some of those whippings they got when they were children. "Tell them about the day you and George smoked cigarettes and the day several of you got into the pan of blue berries."

"Oh, and the Model T Ford truck episode. Don't forget that one." Grandpa Bert said. "Your Daddy did most of the whipping, you told me."

"Yes he did. But now Mother could whip and punish too when the need or occasion arose."

There was a story about Mother having to whip Daniel when he was four years old that Mother told over and over to adults.

One of the restaurant customers who was leaving our property was smoking a cigarette. He threw the half -smoked cigarette down on the ground. Daniel being a 'bad' boy, picked up the cigarette and put the wrong end in his mouth.

He ran up to the house screaming that a bee had stung him. Mother was petting him and rubbing salve on his lips.

Mr. Benson knew what was wrong with that scene because he was the one who had thrown down the cigarette. He knocked on our door and told Mother that a bee had not stung Daniel.

"The wrong end of my cigarette stung him," Mr. Benson told Mother.

Mother turned around and took her small switch out. Daniel's backside got a sting. That's where the salve had to go."

That one got a good chuckle from the kids.

I knew what Grandpa Bert was trying to do. Keep it light for the children.

"I thought maybe Grandpa Bert had forgotten that I told him about one of the first giant whippings that George, Jr. received when he was fourteen years old," I told the kiddies.

I started this story, "Daddy had bought a nearly new pick-up truck. He was so proud of himself that he let the old twenty – five year old model T ford truck take a big rest. He didn't drive it for a while. So, George, Jr thought that Daddy had given up on the old T-truck.

Remember, Daddy had had that truck since his courting days and it was still running or slowly walking. Some old white man had sold that old truck to Daddy for five dollars when Daddy first came to Delaware from Virginia.

The family got tickle on that one, too.

"George, Jr would go out there and mess with that T – truck when he was about fourteen. I told him to leave that truck alone. He sat in it and pretended he was driving it when Daddy wasn't at home. He did that often.'

"One day in the spring, George, tried to start the T- truck. It wouldn't start. He got out and cranked it. He told me to start it. I was scared and didn't try to start it."

"George cranked and cranked, then ran and got back in to start that old rattle trap. He broke the key off in the ignition. He got out and slammed the door of the T -truck and went into the house. No one knew about the T – truck and the key broken but me and George. I was not about to tell on him even though I had warned him."

"Man," said Lil Mike, I sure would liked to have seen that old T truck. I'd have cranked it up, too," he said. "Grandma, you all had some fun in those days. We have never seen a real old truck except in the movie."

"Plus, you didn't tell on each other."

"No, we were loyal to each other. All except Phyllis. She would tell on all of us so she wouldn't get the whipping. Sometime she had done the deed."

"Anyway," I said, "your great uncle George was daring. The T truck had been sitting in the back yard for a while."

One Saturday Daddy decided to crank up the old T truck. He ran in the house hollowing, "who has been messing with my model T- truck?"

"The house got as quiet 'as a rat pissing on cotton," as my old friend Eleanor Miles used to say to me.

"OH, Grandma," said Amelia. OH, Wee!

"AHHH, Granny." Christian- Paris exclaimed. "Are you trying to make us laugh? "Because that sure was funny."

By this time, everyone in the room was laughing, I was trying hard not to laugh.

George got the whipping of his life that night, Daddy figured out who would be bold enough to start up the T- truck without anyone telling him.

"OK, then there was the other smoking episode."

"Grandma, there's another smoking episode?" asked Olivia.

I thought Olivia and the younger children were half asleep.

"Yep." I said. "I think over the years, all of us got caught smoking at one time or another. These were the drastic times when children watched what adults did and tried to emulate them. Smoking looked like fun and a sheer pleasure."

This smoking time was when Mother gave George and me a chore to do."

George, Jr. and I were told by Mother to go into the woods near our house, cut down a Christmas tree and break a grass- sack bag full of holly. It was the twenty -third of December and Mother wanted to decorate our house for Christmas. I was eleven years old and George was about fourteen years old. By now you can surmise that George, Jr and I were pals and hung out together. Where ever he went, he wanted me to go with him.

I remember one time when George was sixteen and I was thirteen, George was driving by then. He wanted me to go with him to see a new girl he met at our high school. George was shy.

When we got to the new girl's house, George just sat there in the car. Finally he got out of the car, knocked on the door and went in to see this new girl that he had just met. She had invited him to come see her on Sunday. She gave George the address.

It was so cold outside. I was sitting in the car shivering for about a half hour, wondering what to do.

"Finally, I got up enough nerve and went and knocked on the door. I went into the house."

George and the new girl were sitting on the sofa.

She asked, "who is that?"

"That's my sister," George answered.

"George, I think you better go," said the new girl.

She thought she had found a new boyfriend. But he had brought his sister.

"The reason I call her 'new girl' is because when George and I got back into Daddy's car, George couldn't remember the new girl's name."

Anyway, back to the Christmas tree. Mother had given us an assignment to cut down a Christmas tree and break a few sprigs of holly for her to make some holly wreaths to put outside on the doors for Christmas.

George had gone to town at some point and bought a pack of cigarettes and a pack of matches. Or one of the older boys may have bought them for him. I didn't know. All I knew was when we got into the woods, George pulled out the pack of cigarettes and lit up one. He gave it to me. I put it to my mouth and started puffing on it.

"Naturally, I didn't know what I was doing."

"Grandma, you should have been a comedian. You tell so many jokes," said Nia.

"Nia, these are not jokes. They may be funny but this is what actually happened when we were children. There was never a dull moment."

I started coughing. George, by this time was smoking a cigarette too. He had stooped over. So I stooped over too. He told me to spit the smoke out. I started spitting which made me cough more.

George patted me on the back thinking it would stop me from coughing. He told me to go sit down on a stomp while he cut the Christmas tree down. He broke off a few sprigs of holly and he said, "Let's go."

Just then, a couple of the bigger older boys came into the woods and started messing with us. We ran out of the woods and went home.

By the time we walked in the door, Mother took one look at me and sent me upstairs to bed. I was wheezing, having an asthma attack. My parents knew that I once and a while had labored breathing and had been diagnosed as being asthmatically prone from allergies and a chronic respiratory disease.

I should grow out of the wheezing and couching as I got older, the doctor reported to my parents. Mother was very careful with me when she heard me wheezing.

George got a whipping that Friday night because Daddy came right in the house and smelled the smoke on him and asked who had been smoking. Daddy didn't say another word. He whipped George with a strap.

Mother didn't tell anything on the little children that evening: that little Hattie had wet the bed a couple of times that week and Nancy had tried to pour molasses on a biscuit and spilled the whole jar of molasses. So George was the only child who got whipped that Friday night. Mother felt that was enough whipping for one night.

Mother came up later and gave me a cup of sassafras tea. It did not have any sugar or milk or anything in it to flavor it. It was nasty tasting. I drank it because Mother was standing over me.

This tea is made from irregularly lobed leaves and aromatic bark. The dried root bark of the sassafras tree is used for flavoring tea and soups and is a source of a volatile oil.

Down south, I learned much later that the native Indians gave us the ground sassafras powder made from the sassafras tree which is called 'file'. It is put in the famous gumbo which is a delicious dish originally made in Africa. File is put into a soup or gumbo to thicken it and give it a delicate flavor.

Mother used sassafras tea whenever we got sick. I hated the taste of it. It was either too sweet or not sweet at all, depending upon the ailment she was treating. I think Mother knew I did not like the tea and that was her way of punishing me so I would not smoke or get into trouble again. It worked.

I went to bed hungry that night. I thought about that many times. Mother did not feed me that night. That was punishment enough.

Much later I was talking to an elderly lady at a program in Chicago. I mentioned this incident to her and said,

"I wonder why my mother sent me to bed without any supper that night."

Mrs. Taylor said, "You know your mother smelt the smoke on your breath, too. She saw that you were sick and she didn't want you to maybe get a whipping too. So she punished you. She couldn't let you get away with it or you would keep on doing bad things."

"Thank you for saying that, Mrs. Taylor. I always felt bad about my mother putting me to bed without any supper," I mused.

"OH, Grandma," said Kiara. "I would have been upset too if my mother put me to bed without eating any dinner."

"Yeah, I survived it. She was wise."

The next big whipping started like this:

"OK. So Daddy brought home a large pail of blue berries one Friday evening. He also brought some bags of cement on the back of his old 1925 model T truck. He put the blue berries in the kitchen sink and said" Some of you come down to the shop and help me unload these bags of cement off the truck. George, Jr and I got up and started walking down to the shop. Daddy was building a grocery "convenient" store. We call them "Mom and Pop Stores" now.

Daniel eventually came down to help us," He told me.

"Daniel told me later in life that he had eaten as many blue berries as Joe had, but he had not gotten a whipping because he was smart enough to come down to the shop and help Daddy."

Daddy apparently did not recognize that Daniel had blue berry stains on his mouth. Daniel was very dark skinned and the stains did not show.

Our adult children and grandkids started laughing. I guess they remembered some of their whippings. They also remembered how much fun Uncle Daniel was with them before he passed.

I said, "when we were through unloading the cement bags, Daddy told us we were going to get an extra 'helping' of ice cream for working with him. He told us to hop on the back of the truck."

I was about nine years old and George, Jr was twelve. Daniel was eight years old.

When we walked into the house, Daddy saw that his large dish pan of blue berries was almost eaten up. He said, "Who ate the blue berries?"

Joe, who was light complexioned and seven years old, and always hungry had blue berries all over his face and lips.

Joe said, "Not me, Daddy. It wasn't *nonna* me. Phyllis gave them to me."

He started crying because he was getting scared of a whipping.

Daddy said, "Joe, it was you. You have blue berries all over your face."

Joe got scared and said, "Daddy, it was Phyllis," he said again. She gave them to me. I thought they were hers."

All my grandchildren and children started laughing and could not stop. They knew they had been in similar situations and could not talk their way out of it.

Granddaddy Bert laughed, too. He said," you've told me that story many times and I can't believe how dumb my brother-in law-Joe was when he was little."

"Bert, he was only a small child as far as my parents could see and had had some mishaps in his young life. Remember he was scolded when he was only two years old and stayed in the hospital two days. That traumatized him maybe for life. He was petted by both Mother and Daddy in those days."

In fact, Mother came downstairs that night of his big whipping and hollered, "don't hurt him, George. He's only a baby."

Yes, he was the youngest boy and Mother petted him and held him a lot. She couldn't get over the fact that we all thought Joe was going to die from being scalded when he was only two years old.

Nancy's Birth

Here comes another part of my family story that I put in my mental diary.

Nancy was being born that fateful day when Joe had that horrific accident. Daddy was outside chopping fire wood for the old wood stove so that he and my grandparents could cook dinner for the family.

Here's how the accident happened. Grandmom Sadie was holding Joe in her arms. The electric coffee pot was percolating. We had electricity in our new house. Grandmom Sadie did not have electricity in her old colonial style home at the Fountain homestead. Nor did Grandmom Hattie have electricity at her two story house in Virginia.

Joe reached around Grandmom Sadie and pulled on the coffee pot plug. He was trying to determine what the noise was. He apparently had not listened to the coffee pot percolating before.

Joe started screaming. Daddy ran into the house to assess the situation. He wrapped Joe in a blanket and cranked up his old 1925 Model T truck.

Joe had scalded himself. Thank God he didn't get Grandmom Sadie, too. That would have been even more tragic and disastrous to scold Grandmom Sadie.

"Yes, before you ask, Daddy had to crank that old truck."

He carried Joe to the hospital eleven miles away. Joe was screaming all the way. They stayed two days and two nights in the hospital."

Daddy had missed the birth of Nancy. She was two days old when Daddy and Joe got home from the hospital.

The three older children, Phyllis, George, Jr and I knew the family was in crisis. Nancy was being born that day before. Joe and Daddy were in the hospital. Grandmom Hattie came out of the small bedroom to tell us that we had a new baby sister. She was named for Mother's favorite aunt, Nancy Harper. I knew before I saw Nancy that she was going to be my very best friend.

I was sandwiched in between these three brothers, one older and two younger. I had an older sister who was already bullying me. I was five and Phyllis was almost ten. That should not have mattered, but it did.

I needed a sister. It turned out that Nancy and I were always close. When she needed something from me, I gave it to her. When I needed something from her, she gave it to me.

Mother liked that. She wanted us all to be close and take care of each other.

The day Nancy was born, Grandmom Hattie came out of bedroom to check on the bigger children. Phyllis and George were in the dining room sitting down eating crackers that Grandmom Sadie had given them. Three year old Daniel was in the kitchen eating a sandwich.

Grandmom Hattie was trying to account for all the children.

"Where is Marian?" Grandmom Hattie asked. The other children did not know.

Grandmom Hattie came into the bathroom and found me on the floor under the large flute footed tub, crying.

"Why are you crying?" she said.

"Whenever you leave the room, tell someone where you are going," she scolded. "We were worried about you and I was looking all over for you."

Grandpa Bert said, "You have told us about your Grandmother Hattie's words of wisdom."

"Mother, I've heard you say that many times. Always tell someone where you are going. Let someone know you are in the vicinity or where you are going, even if it is just out of the room into another room.

"Actually, I didn't always do that," said Karen.

"OH, I know, Karen, you were my devious child. I was always looking for you, in the house, outside, down the street."

"One day when you were in ninth grade and riding the bus to high school, I looked all over for you when I got home from work. I went next door to Ron's house and you were not there. Ron told me you rode around the corner with the other kids who got off the bus on the back streets. We finally found you standing outside one of the other kid's house. The two of you were trying to solve all the problems of the world."

"But your Daddy didn't let you get away with that. He gave you a tongue lashing and then I lit in on you. 'Always tell someone where you are going,' I said.

Keith, Karen's husband, had a good chuckle at that one.

Karen said, "Mother, don't tell my child, Christian-Paris that. He's tough enough to raise as it is."

"Karen, your child is already like you in that respect. Whenever he came to stay with us, I spend half my time looking for him. He uses the three bedrooms that your father and I don't sleep in. One, he spreads out his clothes, one he spreads out his mechanical and technical toys, and one he sleeps on top of, under a quilt. I have to go in every bedroom until I find him."

"Boy is it a joy to have him over, because I get my exercise. Whatever!"

"OH, Granny," said Christian-Paris and laughed.

My grandmother Hattie taught that to me when I was five years.

"When you walk out of the room, tell someone where you are going."

"I told Grandmom Hattie I was praying for Mother and Nancy," I said. After she gave me a good scolding.

Victoria said, "Grandma, you prayed all the time when you were little?"

"Yes, I did. Mother taught me to pray in secret and the Lord will reward you openly. I guess she was talking about the Pharisees and did not want me to be sac-religious.

"Much water has gone under the bridge since then."

"Well, back to Joe. Joe was greedy. He loved to eat. When he comes to our house from North Carolina, he thinks that the whole pot of gumbo that I've made belongs to him. He wants to dip his own bowl of gumbo so he can get all the crabmeat and shrimps. I have to dip it for him," I said.

Christian-Paris said, "Grandma, I remember when we went to Disney world in Orlando, Florida last year. Uncle Joe and Aunt Barbara and their grandchildren came from their apartment to our apartment to our gumbo party the first night. Uncle Joe got mad with you because you fed the children first."

"I was tired from driving back from Disney World but I could see Joe was not going to play fair, so I dipped everyone a bowl of gumbo, children first," I said.

"I remember that', said Amelia Grai. 'Uncle Joe had two big spoons in both hands. He was banging on the counter."

"I want some gumbo, I want some gumbo. Mess with me and I'll go back home," Joe chimed.

"Me too," said Victoria. "I remember him banging on the table and we all started laughing because we were eating gumbo and he wanted some of it. Uncle Joe was so silly and funny. He started laughing, too. I love Uncle Joe. I love his grandchildren, too. They are my cousins."

"Grandma, you are our oral historian. You remember everything, don't you," Kiara our seventeen year old granddaughter mused.

"You remember when you were born. I can't remember a thing about when I was born. I'm glad they took pictures of me so I could know what I looked like when I was a baby"

"Well, I'm sure that remembering one's birth is unusual. But I realized that I had an angel from the day I was born," I said.

"I was above my mother and my two grandmothers, Sadie and Hattie who were both mid-wives."

I wrote a story about that fateful day in 2000 while I was still serving as an administrator and counselor at Southern University. I put it aside because it was so preposterous, I felt no one would believe me.

"I was sitting in the beauty shop one day recently. There were several elderly ladies getting their hair done. We were all talking about old times." I'm old too, but I wasn't as old as they were."

I started telling them about my birth/death experience. One old lady named Patsy said "Don't tell that story anymore. Go home and write it down before you lose it."

"I did, just the first part of the story. Every time I see Patsy at the beauty shop, we chat and we remember a little more of our life stories. She's a joy to talk to.

Sometimes, Elaine, our beautician says, "You all hush, I'm trying to hear my stories. We listen to her stories (Soap Operas) even if we don't want to." She's the one working.

"The story about my birth/death, I'm taking a chance on you guys, my grandchildren. I feel a special bond with each of you. Little children understand some things better than adults. Or they just have more faith."

Jesus had a special closeness with children and told his disciples not to hinder the children.

Jesus said, "Let the children come to me for such as these are in the kingdom of heaven. You cannot get into heaven unless you come as a little child. (Matt. 19:4 NIV)

That is why we as adults try to teach you about Jesus when you are very young."

"You got off the subject again, Grandma," said Nia

"Back to the birthday and the twin brothers. Wow! This is a whopper!"

"Mother told daddy that night when I was two, "Marian sees things. She has premonitions. She sees things before they happen and she sees things after they happen. She may even be seeing ghosts."

Mother told Daddy, "I was like that. I would tell my parents things that would happen and I did not know where I got it from."

Mother told Daddy that she had envisioned her youngest uncle, Sylvester Fountain drown and Grandmom Sadie could not understand Mother's dream or premonition until it happened.

Great uncle Sylvester died at an early age due to a drowning accident in a ditch near the Fountain homestead. Mother saw water floating on the ceiling in her bedroom a few nights before the drowning.

Mother was just a child.

Grandmom Sadie was puzzled. Her mother, great grandmother Amanda Fountain had just died in 1920 in child birth. I found her death certificate on Ancestry.com which stated that she died on November 26, 1920. The cause of her death was toxemia and collapse of the uterus. That meant that Amanda apparently died in childbirth. She lost a baby and died herself. The baby's birth and death were not recorded.

The death certificate had two different spellings of Amanda's last name. The top line was spelled Founting. The bottom line was spelled Fountain (the correct spelling). The death certificate was signed on November 28, 1920 by M. C. Watson, State of Delaware Bureau of Vital Statistics.

Amanda and John Henry Fountain's youngest living son Sylvester was a young child around ten years old and was recorded as living in the household with his parents, according to the 1910 United States Federal Census Record.

Nia, a very astute young person said, "there were many mistakes made on records a long time ago, Grandma. They were costly then and they will be costly now.

"That is correct, Nia."

"Very few records were kept for blacks in those days. It is still difficult to trace our heritage and find out who we really were born to, how many children were lost in childbirth, and when and where they were born. Our families are fortunate because on both sides of the line, they stayed put pretty much and were able to keep better records then most blacks. We always had oral history and tradition to remind us of our heritage."

"It has been in the last century that Blacks have been able to trace our heritage and keep better records and yet there is still much confusion and misunderstanding about black families' births and deaths. I have been tracing our family roots for over fifty years with oral history of my grandparents. I have only recently had breakthroughs with Ancestry.com, the United States Federal Census Record Report, Family source, death certificates, marriage certificates and military draft papers. Not so much success with birth certificates because often time mid-wives could not write or spell names.

Records of property and who owns it is even more arduous and challenging. The property at the Fountain homestead belongs to the descendants of the Fountains and Harpers.

I recently found a 'will' handwritten by Nicholas Fountain from Ancestry, com. There were several Nicholas Fountaine or Fountain. He left the stretch of property in Middleford to Mary Fountain and her son when he became of age.

I believe that was Mary Elizabeth Fountain and her son John Henry Fountain who was Sadie Fountain Harper's Father.

The heirs included Grandmom Sadie and her family. Great Uncle Sylvester, Amanda and John Henry Fountain's youngest son was raised by Grandmom Sadie at the homestead. He and Mother and Uncle Clarence were the last descendants before us, their children.

Uncle Clarence never had any children. However, he married a lady named Lucille who had three college aged children when they married. Uncle Clarence never had the opportunity of raising any children.

Grandpop Herbert, by word of mouth, left a 'will' for Uncle Clarence before he died in 1956. "Never sell the Fountain homestead because it is heir property," he said.

Uncle Clarence broke that promise and sold one piece of the property to a white lady. He had the old colonial home moved and torn down. It hurts me every time I go home to Middleford and note that a century old home is no longer in place. At least, you children have seen the Fountain homestead property.

Much of the assets are gone from the property including the walnut trees, the fruit trees and the old horse barn. Grandpop used to take us for walks in the woods and roam the fields of corn and look at the horses and pigs. He kept one horse tied to a tree near the house because the horse was blind and it was great Grandfather John Henry's favorite horse as he too was blind.

Their descendants still live there.

Moving on, I recently was sent Grandpa Bert's grandmother's birthdate on an old brown piece of paper from a large Griffin family Bible. It was sent to me by Rose Kelly, Grandpa Bert's first cousin. I was astatic.

"Back to my side of the family. Grandmom Sadie and her family were still living in Philadelphia. Their apartment and business caught on fire. They returned home to the Fountain homestead around the time of Great Grandmother Amanda's illness and death.

Sylvester's mother, Amanda died that year and he was left for his oldest sister, Grandmom Sadie to raise with her two children, Lettie and Clarence. Uncle Clarence thought Sylvester was his older brother not his uncle. Grandmom Sadie apparently did not see fit to tell Uncle Clarence that was not his brother. It did not matter. The three children, Great uncle Sylvester, Mother, Lettie and Uncle Clarence were all raised on the Fountain homestead by Grandmom Sadie and Grandpop Herbert. The research about uncle Sylvester Fountain came much later from The United States Federal Census Report of 1910.

This report revealed that in 1910, there were three persons living in the Fountain house whole: John H. Fountain, Father, Amanda C. Fountain, Wife and Sylvester Fountain, son. Grandmom Sadie came home to the Fountain homestead later from Philadelphia after their home and grocery store burned down to the ground.

After Daddy heard Mother's accounts about my having premonitions, dreams and visitations by angels just as Mother had as a child, Daddy started sitting with me and asking me questions.

"How did you see your twin brothers and how do you know that we are going to have two more boys?" Daddy asked me.

"It was extremely bright. I was an infant. I was in heaven" I told Daddy.

"My angel and Jesus told me when I was in heaven to go back because my family needed me." My angel flew me back and I watched my two grandmothers from up high. I was floating with my angel. Grandmom Sadie was holding me after I was born. Grandmom Hattie was on her knees praying and holding Mother's hand. Daddy, you were in the kitchen crying. Grandpop Herbert had come to your house and he was sitting in the yard with Phyllis and George, my two older siblings," I said.

Grandmom Sadie washed my face and laid me on my mother's breast. Mother looked at me and smiled. She kissed me on the cheek and forehead. I touched Mother's face with my fist. Mother started singing softly" Jesus loves me. "I had heard my angel sing that song," I said.

"Then Grandmom Sadie left the bedroom and went outside to get the white wash in. She had washed the sheets and pillow cases the day before on the old wash board and hung them out to dry and catch the sun. The sun bleached them white. Today we buy bleach in the store to get our white clothes clean and white and we put them in an electric dryer. My mother and grandparents didn't have that luxury," I mused.

My grandparents, Sadie and Herbert, walked the mile home and took Phyllis and George with them. They wanted to cook a good meal for everyone. They also wanted to get some relief from the drama of my birth scene. They went to the Fountain homestead.

Olivia said, "Grandma, you always mention the Fountain homestead. Where is that and what is it?"

The Fountain homestead is in Middleford, Delaware. The home has been in our family for over two hundred years. It was built by my great great grandparents, John Henry and Amanda Collins Fountain. My great great grandfather John Henry Fountain was born a slave but was freed by his grandfather, William Fountain who was white. John's mother, Mary Elizabeth Fountain looked white but she was born to a young black slave girl and her white slave master, Nicholas William Fountain. I was given this information from my Grandmom Sadie and my mother. Several years ago

I started searching on Ancestry.com and got more information about my ancestors.

I found death certificates of my grandmother Sadie and grandfather Herbert's on Ancestry.com. Their marriage certificate was found in the Fountain homestead attic. Our grandparents were married on August 6, 1904 in Philadelphia, Pennsylvania by a magistrate. They had two children, both born in Philadelphia. Mother was born on December 6, 1908. Uncle Clarence was born on February 2, 1919.

Big Mike said, "Olivia, remember last year in July when we went to Washington, D.C. to see African American Museum of History and Culture and then to New York to see your friend in the *Lion King*. Then we dropped down to Delaware to see Uncle Albert and Aunt Nancy. They live on the Fountain homestead.

Christian-Paris said, "I wish I had known your mother and your grandmothers. I Love grandmothers." I did go to the Fountain homestead several times to see Aunt Nancy and Uncle Albert.

"Grandma, that time when you and my mother Karen went to New York to sing at Carnegie Hall, Granddaddy Bert and Uncle Albert drove us up there and then we came back to Middleford. I did not know that was the Fountain homestead. I was only three years old," said Christian-Paris.

"We rode and rode all day. I did not know where we were. I just sat in the back seat and sang," said Christian-Paris. We stopped and ate hamburgers and drank sodas. Granddaddy Bert and Uncle Albert talked and talked and talked. I went to sleep and woke up and they were still talking.

It was fun being up there on the Fountain homestead. We roamed the fields and walked in the woods behind Uncle Albert's and Aunt Nancy's house. I enjoy my grandparents and all the old folks," said Christian-Paris.

Christian-Paris' out of body experience

"When my mother and I got back home in Houston, I went to my kindergarten school. I was on the school yard playing kick ball with my playmates. Suddenly I felt something over me, 'a presence'. I stood transfixed, I could not move. I was over myself looking down at myself and my playmates," Christian-Paris said.

"Remember, I told you about it, Grandma when I saw you again."

"I remember, Christian -Paris. I pondered what you said to me. But I don't think you told me the whole story. I could not figure it out. What else happened?"

"Well I could not have been dreaming. I was standing up on the playground playing with my friends. Now I think it was an "out of body experience.""

Christian-Paris had a fleeting moment that he described as an "out of body experience." I was wondering where he got the notion of having an *out of body experience.*

He stated having something or someone hovering over his head. He was looking down on himself and his friends. He was about three years old. He was told to be good to others, especially his friends, his parents and those less fortune than himself.

Christian-Paris said, "I had not thought about it again until now. Someone was talking to me. I think I was seeing my angel. She was flying with me. I was happy."

Christian-Paris realized that he had an angel to guide him at an early age. He was miraculously touched by a 'presence'.

Puzzled, Victoria asked, "What is a 'presence,' Grandma?"

"Let me try to explain it this way," Victoria. "I recently read this book."

Amy Cuddy, in her book, Presence, says, "we know it when we feel it, we know it when we see it. But 'presence' is hard to define." P. 13.

'Presence,' is when all your senses agree on one thing at the same time," stated Majid, United Arab Emirats. "When we are truly present in a challenging moment, our verbal and nonverbal communication flows."

When I heard Christian-Paris discuss his three year old experience, I thought, "My God, what a heavy load for a small child."

But God knew what he was doing. He chose who he wanted to carry out his mission.

Now Christian-Paris is a boy scout, has been for seven years, since he was ten years old. He is now preparing to do his last phase for his eagle scout badge. He is a brilliant student. We are equally proud that his early life experience has lead him up this moment. His project is to upgrade the Ronald McDonald House landscaping in Monroe, Louisiana.

Christian-Paris appealed to his church members at St Mark United Methodist Church to help him raise the money to support his project. After his speech of explaining what the purpose of the Ronald McDonald house was, the congregation was so impressed, he raised money exceeding the amount that he needed for his project.

"It was all good, all good," Christian-Paris said.

Christian-Paris exhibits a quiet strength. He doesn't always talk much or share his feelings.

"Cree-Pete" (my private nickname for Christian-Paris), I feel blessed that you can talk about your feelings and experiences with us. It is obvious that you trust us as a family. You are an only child. It is sometimes challenging and hard to relate to others when you don't have a close relative like a brother or a sister to sound off on. Thank you for sharing your beginnings and accomplishments with us," I said.

"As you say", It's all good," said Christian-Paris.

Michael Gerard II's Physical Reminders

Lil Mike (my nick name for my other grandson, Michael, II) wanted to share some of his experiences with us.

"I have had things and junk happen to me that I still wonder about. I didn't waste time to figure it out when I was small. When I was little, I just ran into Mom and Dad's room and got in the bed with them.

"What happened to you, Mike?" asked Nia. She started laughing.

"It might not be funny, Nia," said Kiara. "Some things that happen are not funny. What happened to you, Mike?

Lil Mike said, "Sometimes now I feel something touch me or come over me, I wake up and don't see anybody so I run to my sisters' room and get in the bed with Victoria."

Lil Mike said, "I just feel tired all the time."

"I remember you told me at your tennis tournament in Baton Rouge that you were so tired, Lil Mike," I said.

"But you did play ping pong after one of your tennis matches. I thought you should have been resting, but you carried on with that ping pong game with James and William. Then you had another tennis match."

Trying to lighten the atmosphere, I said, "Lil Mike, someone once said,

"When you feel dog tired and moody at night, it might be because you've growled all day."

Everyone in the den laughed, not at Lil Mike but at themselves. Lil Mike laughed too.

"Grandma, You are so funny. I like It when we come here to your house," said Olivia.

I said, "reminders of a day gone by may frighten us or have a profound emotional effect on us especially when we awaken from a good or bad dream. Many children are afraid of the dark and the unknown. And the dark and night time hold the unknown in its hand."

There is a thin line between good and evil. There is a thin line between love and hate. I didn't make that up. I heard it somewhere a long time ago in one of my psychology classes," I pronounced.

"I do know this for a fact and have taught it to each of you as well as other children. Middle C on a piano is the dividing note. This is the first note on the piano that you learn because it is the dividing note. Some things that you are afraid of are not bad. It is just your feelings that get you all mixed up inside and make you apprehensive," I said.

"Joyce Meyer stated in her book, *Living Beyond Your Feelings*," that we all have days (or nights) when we feel more emotional than other days and there may be many reasons why. Perhaps you didn't sleep well the night before, or you ate something that lowered your blood sugar or something that you are allergic to. The occasional emotional day is something we don't have to be concerned about, Lil Mike. Just say 'this too shall pass," P. 17.

Meyers goes on to say," Sometimes we feel emotional because something upset us the day before and we didn't resolve it. We are often guilty of stuffing things down inside us rather than dealing with them. If you are a person who avoids confrontations, you can have a soul full of unresolved issues that need closure before emotional wholeness can come." P. 18.

"Grandma," said Nia, "Where do you find all these sayings in these books?"

"Nia, I ask God for help so I can help others. He sends books and things my way."

"Lil Mike and all of you, in facing issues, Jesus gave us the first principle to remember concerning stable emotional health.

He said "You will know the truth and the truth will set you free." (John 8: 32 NIV).

"Life is not always fair, but God is. Always remember that blaming someone else for what's happening to you does not help you enjoy freedom and wholeness. I encourage you to not get stuck in a time frame in your life," I said.

Lil Mike continued to explain, "I get so tired when I play in the band and my legs start hurting and I don't feel like coming home and doing my home work and house work. I get real cranky and feel like every one is picking on me."

Lil Mike, "You're going to have to communicate some of these things to your parents, that your legs and body are hurting and your feelings are hurt, too. Sounds like you need some 'muscle rub' for your aching legs and body."

"I'm old so I use muscle rub to my heart's content. You're young, but you still have to take care of your body. It belongs to God. You don't get but one body, maybe a few extra body parts, but only one body."

"I agree wholeheartedly to Meyer's statement and add that you are one of God's children. You are no better or no worse than anyone else in the world," my mother always told us.

"Every morning and evening, I repeat a verse that I learned when I was a small child:

"The Lord is my Shepherd, I shall not want. He leads me in the path of righteousness for his namesake. (Ps.23:1-3 NIV).

"Lil Mike, all children need encouragement for them to succeed in life. It leaves a very powerful effect on their lives when they do get encouragement and support."

Let me paraphrase a story that I read in Dan Walch's book, *The Promise.*

A man named Jim told his nephew that he kept flunking math because his teacher never encouraged the class and always put the failing students that he called dumb in the back of the classroom.

When a new teacher, Mr. Fowler, was sent to that class, he told his students "If anyone fails in this class, then I have failed." p.325.

He tutored students or did whatever it took to make math fun and interesting. At the end of the school year, Mr. Fowler posted all the grades outside the classroom on the door for the children to see.

Many of us had been failing under our other teacher. Mr. Fowler pledged to see that we learned math and enjoyed it. We all passed math that year. Encouragement and diligence, that's what it took.

Jim realized later in life that the first teacher was just like his dad, never encouraging him or his siblings: never an encouraging word. It's something we as children crave and long for but so few of us ever receive praise. Children feel bad and go through torment when they don't get the praise and love they need from their parents. They grow up crippled and feel picked upon.

Jim had several younger siblings. When he was an only child, he received much attention from his parents and other family members.

When other siblings were born in the family, Jim got less and less attention from home and started failing in school. Parents don't always realize the detriment that is caused when a child is seeking attention and the parents are not aware of the child's needs, which often leads to scolding and chastisement.

"The child may be the victim through no fault of his or her own." Walch, p.326.

"Grandma, sometimes I feel like Jim did." said Lil Mike.

"I was the cat's meow when I was younger and didn't have any sisters. Now I get yelled at and hollowed at all the time. I don't have any brothers, so I wonder if it's because I am a boy."

Lil Mike, Walch also stated that "Changing things on the outside can't fix problems in our heart."

"That's like a dog running away trying to get away from its fleas. The dog doesn't realize that the fleas goes where ever he goes." P.190.

In other words, our problems follow us. Sometimes when you talk at someone whom you have a close relationship with instead of talking to the individual, you create or magnify your problem.

"With this in mind, there is always the possibility of having nightmares and other bad dreams. You are not resolving your relationship issues," I said.

"You have to hit the reset button to find what is wrong with the relationship. Sometimes, you have to be the adult in the room," I said.

"Your parents are loving and kind. Find a way."

"Have you sat down and tried to say that to your parents. Tell them how you feel in a gentle way, because they have feelings and emotions too. Remember I said earlier that it's bad when you keep your emotions bottled up inside. Then at night you have nightmares and other emotional issues," I said.

Michael and Tracie were quietly listening. I was hoping they were listening with their heart as well as their ears. Their only son was hurting.

I was not trying to use my counseling skills on Lil Mike but he was revealing his feelings and I was attempting to explore ways of closing the gap between parents and child.

"Wow! Ma, we are learning quite a bit today," Michael, my son said. Are we going home with an ear full!"

"Children, are you ready to go home?" asked Tracie.

Olivia replied, "No I want to hear who my great grandmother was."

"Just one more little story, Grandma," said Victoria.

"OK, Guys", I said. "One more little story."

CHAPTER IV

MY MOTHER LETTIE - INCREDIBLE

Victoria chimed, "Grandma, tell us about your mother. What did she look like. What was she like?"

"Wow! I was afraid you would never ask. I can give you a quick version of my mother, but it will not do her justice."

"Go ahead, Ma," said Bertrand, II. I need to hear this. You gave our children stands of picture books so we know what our grandparents and even our great grandparents look like.

Well, here goes:

Lettie – Mother was who she was. I went and got several pictures of Mother and showed the kiddies my album. The most precious one of all is a picture of my mother and father dressed in formal wear and leaning against each other. In that picture, they had attended a Masonic cotillion ball where I was one of the young maidens to the cotillion Queen. – that's incredible.

Lettie - When I met my mother Lettie, she was a beautiful fair complexion, five feet tall, thirty year old woman. I met her at my birth. She was the only daughter of Grandpop Herbert and Grandmom Sadie Harper. She was well loved by her parents and her grandparents – that's incredible.

Lettie – Was an only child for ten and a half years. Yet she accepted her infant brother, Clarence and helped to care for him even though she too was a young child. She was giving and loving, especially to her only brother. Even after Mother and her younger brother had their own home and families, I remember Lettie and Clarence celebrating every holiday together with their families. – that's incredible.

Lettie - A black woman born on December 6, 1908, attended elementary school in Philadelphia, Pennsylvania, middle school in Middleford, Delaware, a boarding school - high school in Rocky Mount, North Carolina, received her first college degree in music from Cheyney University in Cheyney, Pa. and received her second college degree in education from Delaware State University -all this by the time she was twenty-two years of age- that's incredible.

Lettie – Mother was smart, in fact, brilliant, imaginative, prayerful, compassionate and dedicated to her parents, loving to her husband and children, courageous and kind and a blessing to all she met. Yet she was humble. - that's incredible.

Lettie – She was and still is our super hero. My siblings and I always speak of how she raised us. – that's incredible.

Lettie -By the time she was still a teenager, she was an accomplished pianist and played for an accomplished contralto singer, Marian Anderson for two years. – that's incredible.

Lettie - After she completed college, she played jazz in bars in Wilmington, Delaware, played hymns and gospel music in churches all over Delaware and the mid-Atlantic states, played for school programs, formed a quartette of her own four oldest children, taught music in her private home to her own children and neighbor's children, wrote music and articles for local newspapers – that's incredible.

Lettie – followed after her parents as far as being an educator, proprietor and a philanthropist. Mother's parents owned a grocery store in Philadelphia when mother was a small child. Their grocery store and apartment caught on fire and burned to the ground. - that's incredulous.

Lettie - When they returned to Delaware, they became a part of the underground railroad movement. Yes, slavery was still going on. Mother was about ten years old. She told me that her grandfather, John Henry Fountain told her about the movement. They helped run away slaves and freed slaves to safety by hiding them in their own Fountain homestead, under beds, behind hollowed out dresser drawers and horse barns -that's incredible.

Lettie – She always treated others with respect, kindness and honor no matter what their station or needs in life were. She counseled children and youth, especially pregnant teens, while other adults criticized and made fun of the youths. - that's incredible.

Lettie - Gave birth to fourteen children (seven died), raised seven of those children to be professionals and good people, three sons in the armed services (navy). George, Jr, my oldest brother was one of the first blacks in the navy in the middle fifties. – that's incredible.

Lettie - When her three sons retired from the navy, they went to college or furthered their education and secured professional employment. No jailbird – that's incredible.

Lettie - Daddy told my brothers early in life, "if you get yourself in jail, don't call me because I didn't raise no jailbirds. - that's incredible.

Lettie - The four daughters became college graduates. (Phyllis, the oldest sibling, graduated from technical school) and went on to receive graduate degrees, no jail birds – that's incredible.

Lettie - Mother and Daddy owned their own grocery store and restaurant which she cooked for- this was so she could add resources to the family and could help feed the poor and hungry in our community. – that's incredible.

Lettie - Daddy build our home with mother giving him the first ten dollars out of her piano teaching savings to buy the property. Then he built a restaurant and attached a grocery store and barber shop to the restaurant later. – that's incredible.

Lettie - Mother and Daddy put the first public telephone in their store. Only one or two families had telephones in their homes in the early fifties – that's incredible.

Lettie - It was determined early in life that Mother had a medical problem. She was a juvenile diabetic. Her parents wanted a normal family life for her, education for their children in finer schools, have their own business and above all, be independent from their parents. They were frugal and saved their money and started building their own business and apartment in Philadelphia to have a better life – that's incredible.

Lettie - She was unique as a child, having premonitions and seeing visions, according to Grandmom Sadie, her mother. She grew into an exceptional young woman. Lettie went to school in Philadelphia for five years until she was ten years old – that's incredible.

Lettie - Mother was always reading. She was an avid reader. She wanted us to read – thay's incedible.

Lettie - "Bernard Shaw once said, "If you teach a man anything, he will never learn. You learn by doing. - that's incredible.

Lettie - "Learning is an active process. Only knowledge that is used sticks to your mind," said Dale Carnegie.(p. 186.) -that's incredible.

Lettie – Mother taught by example. She knew how to "win people to her way of thinking. Yet she always tried to see things from the other person's point of view." This was one of Carnegie's principles. – that's incredible.

Lettie – "I get it Grandma," Nia said. - that's incredible.

Lettie – Bertrand, II, Nia's father said, "Ma, I understand what you are saying. You taught by example, also. You used to say, when one moves, we all move. Meaning, let's all clean the house together or lets all get in the car to shop together." – that's incredible.

Lettie – Mother read her Bible every night and Dale Carnegie's book, *How to Win Friends and Influence People* in the day time. That book seemed to be her day time Bible or guide.

She adhered to one of Carnegie's principles: "Try honestly to see things from the other person's point of view". p. 186. – that's incredible.

Lettie – I got infinitely more pleasure from listening to Mother correct herself than to hear her scolding us. - that's incredible.

Lettie - Mother's younger brother, Uncle Clarence was born in Philadelphia about ten months before they left that city. Mother dearly loved her little brother and helped to take care of him. My grandparents were experiencing their dream of owning their own home and business and having a beautiful family. They were happy – that's incredible.

Lettie - Suddenly everything crashed. Their family had to move from Philadelphia that year when Uncle Clarence was born because their store and apartment burned down. Grandmom Sadie and her two children ran for their lives when the house caught on fire - that's incredulous.

Lettie - "Run, Lettie, run," my grandmother yelled. Grandmom grabbed Uncle Clarence who was a ten month old baby and they ran out of the house together losing everything. When Grandpop Herbert came home from work, the family prepared to leave Philadelphia for Middleford right away where the Fountain homestead was – that's incredulous.

Lettie - They were devastated and sad. Grandmom Sadie had wanted to be independent and had moved upstate, got married and built a home and grocery store. The fire created much havoc in their lives. They returned home to the Fountain homestead disappointed and destitute. They had lost all their worldly goods – that's incredulous.

Lettie - I recently read in *Philadelphia Divided* by James Wolfinger "that the Great Migration of World War I and the 1920's brought one million African Americans to the northern states from the south. Between 1910 and

1920, over a hundred and forty thousand blacks settled in Philadelphia – that's incredible.

Lettie - Once in Philadelphia and Chicago, these blacks found few options for housing, jobs or security. There was a struggling economy all over the land. These were uncertain times. There were so many difficult and life altering situations. It took courage, strength and trust in God to try and navigate the future however alarming it looked – that's incredulous.

Lettie - We don't always know the extent of other's trials. "Strife and racial conflicts occurred frequently. Irish settlers who were in housing areas first, then Jews and Italians were competing for better housing and living conditions." Wolfinger, p.13. - that's incredulous.

Lettie - Even though Grandmom Sadie, Grandpop Herbert and their children were living in Philadelphia before many of the whites, their family was subjected to some of the harshness that was being perpetrated upon blacks in general. – that's incredulous.

Lettie - Many black groups were being burned out by hate groups such as the Klan. I doubt that Grandmom Sadie actually knew how the fire in their home was started. My mother and grandparents never told us children that they were intentionally burned out by an arsonist and run out of Philadelphia - that's incredulous.

Lettie - Grandmom Sadie's mother and father were still at the Fountain homestead. That was their home. Great grandfather - John Henry was blind and great grandmother Amanda, "everyone called her Mandy" was ill - that's incredible.

Lettie - Grandmom Sadie immediately took charge of the house because she knew how to run a house whole. She not only had her own two children to raise now. She had her youngest brother, Sylvester to raise along with her two, Lettie and Clarence. There was roughly ten years between each of these three children. that's incredible.

Lettie - Grandmom Sadie made no difference between their three children. Sylvester became her child as well as her own two children. No wonder Uncle Clarence thought Sylvester was his brother instead of his uncle. - that's incredible.

Lettie - "Grandma, you talk about your grandparents and great grandparents as if you know them," said Kiara." - that's incredible.

Lettie - "I did know my grandmother Sadie Fountain Harper and grandfather Herbert Harper but I did not know my great grandparents John

Henry and Amanda Fountain, my grandmother Sadie's parents and Delcey and Steven Harper, grandpop Herbert's mother and father. - that's incredible.

Lettie - I said. "I feel that I knew them because my mother and grandparents talked about them quite a bit. Remember I told you that you learn much about your ancestors through oral history' -that's incredible.

Lettie - "Grandma, you are so incredible when you say, - 'that's incredible or that's incredulous.'

Lettie - "What does incredible and incredulous mean?" asked Lil Mike.

Lettie - "Guys, according to the Webster's II New College Dictionary, 'incredible means astonishing, or too implausible to be believed," I said. "Incredulous goes a step further. It means skeptical, or actually expressing disbelief" that's incredible.

Lettie - I feel that incredible and incredulous is expressing strength against all odds. Combating obstacles and winning - that's incredible.

Lettie - "I learned much from the book that I quoted by Ryan Holiday. This book was written in 2014 but has lifelong philosophy in it" -that's incredible.

Lettie - Holiday wrote "Marcus Aurelius, the emperor of the Roman Empire in the year 170 sat down to write, not for publication but for himself. In Marcus's words is the secret to an art known 'as turning obstacles upside down' that's incredible.

Lettie - His philosophy was to "act with a 'reverse clause' so there is always a way out or another route to get to where you need to go, so that setbacks or problems are always expected and never permanent. Make certain that what impedes us can empower us."(Holiday, p. xiv.) – that's incredible.

Lettie - To this particular man, these were no idle words. Aurelius was faced with wars, a horrific plague, a depleting treasury, repeated and arduous travel across continent and an attempt on the throne by one of his closes allies during his reign of nineteen years. P. xiv – that's incredible.

Lettie - "From what we know he truly saw each and every one of his obstacles as an opportunity to practice some virtue: patience, courage, humility, resourcefulness, reason, justice and creativity. The power he had, never seemed to go to his head-neither did the stress or burden. He rarely rose to hatred or bitterness." P. xv. Lettie was very much like that - that's incredible.

Lettie - The Fountains and the Harpers, both black and white members, apparently had some of the same virtues. They were a part of the Underground Railroad. They could not talk about this to persons they could not trust – that's incredible.

Lettie - They were to remain stationed so they could help others who did not have the same advantages that they had. This extended black family was freed by their white family and given land to build on – that's incredible.

Lettie - "Grandmom Sadie told me when I was seven that her ancestors were from Africa and France. She knew that when the time was right, I would tell their story to the world," - that's incredible.

Lettie - "Grandma, you are some story teller," mused Victoria. "I wish I had lived back in that day. Little Sophia woke up from a nap in her mother, Tracie's lap. Sophia touched Tracie's arms. "I'm hungry," she said. - that's incredible too.

Lettie - Amelia said, "Sophia, you are always hungry, just like Daddy." that's incredible.

Lettie - "Yep, I'm hungry, too," said Big Mike. I'll make hamburgers for lunch, then we can go down to Dookie Chase restaurant for a big supper." that's incredible.

Lettie - "Grandma, you told me once that Grandmother Lettie went away to a boarding school in high school," Christian-Paris reminded me. =that's incredible.

Lettie - "Yes, when your great grandmother Lettie started school in Middleford, the school had only six grades. Mother finished the fifth and sixth grades at the little one room Neal elementary school in a year and a half. There was no high school for black children or white children in Middleford. – that's incredulous

The white children went to another school in another town called Seaford. That school went to the ninth grade. If they wanted to go further, they had to attend a preparatory or a military school. - that's incredible.

Lettie - Mother helped Grandmom Sadie around the house after her school days. She loved her grandparents and helped her grandfather who was blind. He took her to his church one day and she began playing the piano at the old St John Methodist church. Mother's grandfather heard her play and one day brought home a baby grand piano. Mother was so thrilled. She had taken piano lessons in Philadelphia from her school teacher when she was five years old. She furthered her piano skills when she attended boarding school in North Carolina. Mother loved music and wanted to help other children learn to play. She began teaching her little cousins how to play the piano. - that's incredible.

Lettie - Grandmom Sadie realized that Mother was a very astute child, a fast learner ahead of her class because she had attended a primary school in Philadelphia which was more progressive.- that's incredible.

Lettie - Grandpop Herbert had two ministerial brothers, Rev. Robert and Burton Harper. They had founded a boarding school in Rocky Mount, North Carolina. They both taught at the school. - That's incredible.

Lettie -Grandmom Sadie and Grandpop Herbert had a big decision to make. Middleford was an unprogressive rural area, with farm land seen for stretches of miles, outdoor toilets were seen for more miles. This was the order of the day. – That's incredible.

Lettie - Well, it was the early 1920's during my mother's childhood. Mother had never been away from her parents. However, Grandmother Sadie wanted only the best for her only daughter. They decided to sent Mother to the Harper Brother's boarding school. - that's incredible.

Lettie - It was going to be a great sacrifice financially, psychologically and physically. The Fountain and Harper families would miss Mother. However, Grandmom Sadie loved her daughter dearly. She was not to be denied furthering her education. that's incredible.

Lettie - My little mother, Lettie left home at the tender age of thirteen to enter a boarding school with a suit case, coat and hat and flat black shoes. Upon arrival, she was placed in the care of her aunt Nancy. Nancy Harper was the younger sister in the Harper family. She helped Mother to get adjusted and not feel so homesick. - that's incredible.

Lettie - As you can see, our family was thoroughly educational minded. Mother was sixteen upon the completion of her education at the boarding school. After a brief period at home in Middleford, Mother went to Cheyney State University on a family scholarship. This was a privilege to attend a boarding school and then go to college. In two years, Mother graduated from Cheyney State Norman for Colored Girls which was renamed Cheyney University. She majored in classical music. - that's incredible.

Lettie - Mother did not stop there. By this time in 1930, she entered Delaware State College, later named Delaware State University and received a degree in music and education. She was eligible to teach music and education. Wanting to be independent, Mother got a small apartment and was hired to play jazz piano music in a bar in Wilmington, Delaware. - that's incredible.

Lettie - She was given the privilege of playing at a program for Marian Anderson at Cheyney State University. They were both born in Philadelphia, Marian Anderson born on February 17, 1902 and Mother born on December

6, 1908. They became close while really getting to know each other at Cheyney State College(now university). – that's incredible.

Lettie – Mother played for Marian Anderson for two years during and after her college days. I met Miss Anderson when I was thirteen years old. Mother was asked to serve as Anderson's pianist at a Masonic cotillion program in Maryland. - that's incredible.

Lettie – Mother married Daddy. Daddy was in love with Mother. She was unconcerned and living independently and following her chosen career and making her own money. Daddy went to Grandmom Sadie and told her he did not know how to approach Mother.- that's incredible.

Lettie - She was pretty, and educated, yet humble and dedicated to her family. Grandmom Sadie suggested that he write Mother a letter asking to come and see her in Wilmington. She consented. He put his old piece of nineteen twenty- five Model T ford back together and drove as fast as he could from Middleford, Del to Wilmington. That was slow and noisy, I grant you. - that's incredible.

Lettie – Daddy knew that mother was a brilliant woman. During their courtship period, Daddy had no clue as to how to win her over. Mother apparently fell in love with my poor little daddy. They married right away in a small Methodist church and had a small reception on the lawn of the Fountain homestead. - that's incredible.

Lettie – Before Mother got out of college, she played for Marian Anderson in some of her concerts. After college and working for two years, Mother took the option of getting married and having a large family while Marian Anderson, her good friend, went on to fame and fortune. – that's incredible.

Lettie – They had all of us. – that's incredible.

Lettie - Later as I was sixteen years old, Mother sent me to Washington, D.C.to hear Marian Anderson sing the National Anthem at Dwight D. Eisenhower's Inauguration in the late 1950's. My history teacher, Mr. Monroe Hearn from William C. Jason high school chartered a bus from Georgetown, Delaware for our tenth grade class to attend the inauguration that snowy cold day on January 20. I went to hear my name sake sing. Daddy had only enough money to send one child. Mother selected me to go to D.C. - that's incredible.

Lettie - When Marian Anderson stood on the Capital steps and sang the National Anthem, I got off the bus to really hear her. Mr. Hearn was the only other person who stood out there with me. Daddy had sacrificed to send me. I wanted to see and hear everything. - that's incredible.

Lettie - Marian Anderson had launched her career. She was a hit in Germany and England, a famous black contralto singer for all the world. Mother had traveled around with her when Mother finished Delaware State University. They were on a path together around the mid-Atlantic states for about two years in 1932-1933. Marian had sung all over the world by this time. She was honored many times during her career, but her greatest honor and tribute came from legendary conductor, Arturo Toscanini when Marian was beginning her career. - that's incredible.

Lettie - Mother told me, "I admired Marian Anderson so much." – that's incredible

Lettie - Anderson's lowest point in life was when she returned to the United States. She was constantly being discriminated against in the United States because she was black - that's incredulous.

Lettie - When I read my Black Heritage Stamp about Marian Anderson, I learned "that in 1935, legendary Solomon Hurok represented her and scheduled her singing tours in the Soviet Union, which was a great feat. - that's incredible.

Lettie - "For her homecoming back to the United States in the late 1930's, Hurok booked Anderson to a performance in 'Town Hall' and wanted her to sing in Washington D. C. at Constitution Hall." that's incredible.

Lettie - Mother told me that in February 1939, Anderson was refused that honor because she was a black woman. The Daughters of the American Revolution denied Anderson this privilege on racial grounds and her black family and friends were denied entrance to the event. – that's incredulous.

Lettie - Eleanor Roosevelt and the Roosevelt Administration hearing this, stepped in and scheduled Anderson to sing on the steps of the Lincoln Memorial building and she sang to over seventy–five thousand people of all races.—that's incredible.

Lettie - This was on February 28, 1939, the year I was born. Mother and Daddy attended the concert at the foot of the Lincoln Memorial monument that cold day. The concert was played on the radio and many, many other people heard it. Her career took on a new high in the United States. – that's incredible.

Lettie - "Grandma, you have had some great experiences," said Nia. – that's incredible.

Lettie - Christian-Paris said, "Grandma, you are so adventurous. You took the whole family to Washington to see Barack Obama inaugurated on January 20, 2009 and January 20, 2013. It was freezing cold but we huddled together and bore the weather. It was an amazing event both times." said Christian-Paris. that's incredible.

Lettie - 'Grandma, you said that this was a once in a life time experience and you wanted us to participate in this and many other good occasions," said Lil Mike. - that's incredible.

Lettie - "I'm so glad I got to go with Dad," said Lil Mike. We flew up on Thursday and stayed in the Marriott hotel. Then we flew back home to New Orleans after we saw President Obama inaugurated. Man, it was cold and I was so hungry out there, but we had fun," said Lil Mike. - that's incredible.

Lettie - "Grandma, Dad and I walked you back to the Union train station to meet Christian and Uncle Keith and hurried up and walked back to the hotel and got our stuff and took a cab to the airport. Boy, that was something. I'm glad Dad took me," said Lil Mike. - that's incredible.

Lettie - "Me too," said Christian-Paris. "We stayed in Granny's time share in Williamsburg, Virginia and had a ball. We drove up to Washington from Baton Rouge and stayed overnight at our cousin Mary's house in South Carolina. After we arrived at Williamsburg, Virginia, we caught the train and rode into Washington and stayed at the Capital Hotel for one night. We got a suite in that hotel but there were seven of us in that one suite. There was no other room in the inn. It was all good, though. – that's incredible.

Lettie - "Grandma, you said your mother felt this way, too. Get as much education and good things out of life as you can. It will enhance your knowledge and your self-esteem," said Kiara – that's incredible.

Lettie - "Yes, my mother Lettie loved to travel and always encouraged us to 'go see the world for yourself." – that's incredible.

Lettie - Mother was industrious and versatile, as well as flexible. Anyone who can play the piano for a famous contralto singer such as Marian Anderson for over two years, play jazz in bars and play hymns and spirituals in churches is a genius who has exceptional, intellectual and creative power. That was my mother. – that's incredible.

Lettie - My mother also composed songs. She composed and wrote the words to a song called, *That's the Story of,that's the Glory of Love*. Years after she had left Wilmington, Delaware to settle down and raise a family, she sent her song to a man she slightly knew. He said the song was no good. –that's incredulous.

Lettie - Later Mother heard the song being played and sung on the radio. She was puzzled and tried to contact the man she had sent her music to. To no avail, she had no way of asking for help in locating the man who had "taken" her song. - that's incredulous.

Lettie -This was during the period immediate after World War II. The only way of honoring my mother for writing that song is to tell you, my grandchildren and all the world about her composing that song. – that's incredulous.

Lettie – Mother's motto was: work with your head, your heart and your hands. You'll never be broke and you will always do good. – that's incredible.

She was teaching us good work ethics. She was showing us that the what's and the who's were less important than the how's and the why's. – that's incredible.

Lettie - Choose wisely what you want to do in life because we should be more interested in how we work rather than what we do for a living. That is what will make our life's work meaningful. Be dedicated, be honest and be diligent in all that you do. - that's Incredible.

Lettie – Mother was an avid reader and a great musician. She insisted on each of us playing at least one musical instrument and possibly two. I was the only one who continued to play the piano, even though she taught all of us to play. All of my siblings were in the band in high school but me. - that's incredulous.

Lettie - Mother had told our high school music teacher about my breathing problem. So my music teacher did not let me get in the band because he said since I had asthma, I would get too winded and not be able to march in the band. He had me hit a note or two on the piano when we sang a capella -that's incredible.

Lettie – Mother's insisting that I learn to play the piano paid off when I went to college. I received a music scholarship when I attended Delaware State University. – that's incredible.

Lettie – Mother's words and lessons came to fruition many years later in my life. As I was working at Southern University in Baton Rouge as a counselor/administrator, an elderly professor came to me in the Credit Union, saying "You are Daniel Heath's sister, aren't you. I did not really know this professor but I had heard of him in the education department- that's incredible.

Lettie – I said, "Yes, I am," knowing something good was going to come from this conversation – that's incredible.

Lettie – I just met your brother, Danny. He's a student here in engineering. He's not a young student, he's a non-traditional student, been in the navy for twenty- two years. I was in the marines for six years. Any way, he was recommended to me to fix my air conditioner at my house, which he did. We talked. - that's incredible.

Lettie – He told me about you being a professor up here. He also told me that your mother had a strong work ethics and taught all her children to 'work with your head, your heart and your hands and you would never be broke and you will be able to help someone else. – that's icredible.

She would say, "keep working, right now you are working with your hands. Someday you will be working with your head and your heart. You will be doing what you want to do in life. Yes, we did work as children in the fields and in other people's homes which I will tell you more about later. " -that's incredible.

Lettie – Mother not only had a work ethic she had an ethic whereby she could whip or punish us when the need or occasion arose. Yes, she could whip pretty hard, too. That too is another chapter. - that's incredible.

Lettie – "Yes, she did teach us well and taught us to be humble no matter what type of work we did," I said. _ That's incredible.

Lettie – "Daniel is taking one of my education courses as an elective," Dr Wallace told me. "I teach it every semester." That' incredible.

Lettie - "I would like to invite you to take this free for credit and would also help you to get a scholarship to attend Kansas State University to work on your PH.D. -that's incredible.

Lettie – Daniel told me that your mother went to boarding school and college at a very early age and that your grandfather and great uncles went to Bible school. – that's incredible.

Lettie – "Your mother wanted all her children to finish high school which they did. She wanted at least four of you to attend college. The three boys wanted to join the navy and did. – that's incredible.

Lettie - I was sandwiched in between those three brothers and wanted to join the navy and travel, too. My male chauvinistic siblings told me that I could not get into the navy. I did not join and I am glad I didn't. - that's incredible.

Lettie - I accepted the offer to take his class in Drug Abuse Education. I took a follow -up course in that area paid for by my sorority. This course was taught by a group of teachers at the Red Cross building.- that's incredible.

Lettie – I had a conversation with my husband and three children about accepting the offer to attend Kansas State University. Both my children and my husband needed me at home at that time, so I did not accept that offer. I really wanted to go work on my PHD. – that's incredible.

Lettie – Daniel and Dr. Wallace apparently talked much. Dr. Wallace mentioned Daniel often to me. – that's incredible.

Lettie - "Daniel is a good smart man and your mother was apparently a good person. She wanted only the best for her children " – that's incredible.

Lettie – Being educational minded paid off. All of Lettie's children received a good education. All of Lettie's grandchildren, our children and nieces and nephews, received a college education, now it is time for you, our grandchildren. We are so proud of you.

"Nia, you are in college, Kiara, your turn is this fall. Christian – Paris, your time is next Fall. Then here come all my little ones." – that's incredible.

Lettie – I did follow up on Dr. Wallace's offer to take that free class and numerous other courses. I finished my third masters degree in mass communication and journalism at Southern University. - that's incredible.

Lettie – I worked all day at Southern University and attended classes three nights a week until I finished that degree. – that's incredible.

Lettie – "And Grandma, you are trying to make sure that all of your grandchildren get their college degrees," said Christian Paris. -that's incredible.

Lettie – "Yes," I said. "I have started an educational IRA for each of you grandchildren to help defray your college fees. _ that's incredible.

Lettie - "Nia and Kiara, you two are receiving your *Griffin scholarships now as you are in college. – that's incredible.*

Lettie – Well to make a long story short…..," I began. – that's incredible.

Lettie- "And we love you, Grandma," said Victoria. – that's incredible.

Lettie – Your great grandmother, Lettie always gave bountifully of what she had. She made sure that she shared with everyone she met and that she had plenty to give. - that's incredible.

Lettie – I told you there was much more to Lettie than the eyes could see. Mother planted two gardens each season: one in the spring with Kale, squash, peas, cucumbers, tomatoes, and one in the fall: collard greens, corn, sweet potatoes, white potatoes and peanuts that had to be dug up out of the ground. – that's incredible.

Lettie – We always had plenty to eat and the neighbors did too. Mother sold a few vegetables in her store and gave away a lot. She could not see anyone go hungry. She would say, "if I could feed the whole world, I would." She sent food to the soldiers who came home crippled and the children who went to school hungry. – that's incredible.

Lettie – Vegetables were not the only crops. We had pear trees, cherry trees, black walnut trees (at Grandmom Sadie's house), watermelons, loaded grape vines and strawberries. We picked wild blackberries and blueberries from the woods behind our house near the railroad tracks. There were apple orchards and peach orchards out in the countryside that mother let us go and pick for pay, my three brothers and me. – that's incredible.

Lettie - The two little girls, our youngest sisters, Nancy and Hattie Elviria, were too small to let out the house without Mother. Phyllis was always upstairs reading. Mother let her study. We children were allowed to bring home bushels full of fruit in the summer after we had picked all day for a few coins. Daddy met us in his old model T ford truck to bring the produce and fruit home. This too, Mother sold a few in her grocery store and gave away a lot. – that's incredible.

Lettie – We lived near the water. We were right on the Atlantic ocean and the Chesapeake Bay. Often Daddy went out on the boat at night in Maryland and caught fish with the other fishermen. He also bought tubs of oysters, crabs and shrimp which he brought home for mother to cook for our restaurant and us – that's incredible.

Lettie - There again, if a man came into the restaurant on Saturday afternoon and did not have a quarter to buy an oyster fritter, she would tell him to enjoy the oyster fritter and pay her later, knowing that he would not have a quarter the next Saturday, either. – that's incredible.

Lettie – Mother believed and taught us that if and when challenges of life cut you down, God restores and renews you through others. She also believed in the Lord's prayer:

> "Our Father which art in heaven, Hallowed be thy name. Thy kingdom came. Thy will be done on earth as it is in heaven. Give us this day, our daily bread. And forgive us our debts, as we forgive our debtor. (Matt. 6: 9-13, KJV). -that's incredible.

Lettie – I used to enjoy hearing Daddy say, "Marian is always helping out or Marian will be the salvation of us all. One day as a young adult, I realized that I received undo praise because Mother always taught me to stay out of trouble, don't let anyone rule your mind. Think for yourself. Go away and make your own way. - that's incredible.

Lettie – Now I am coming full circle. As circumstances change, I realize or discern that one has to get involved, get your hands dirty, get in the mud with someone else and don't worry about praise. What Mother taught me was: is that all there is to life? - that' s incredible.

Lettie – Sometimes I wonder, am I guilty of accepting undeserved admiration and credit for my 'so called' clean life. It's easy to give the impression of being virtuous; simply do nothing difficult, controversial or upsetting to people. This is what Mother taught me, isn't it? - that's incredible.

Lettie – "But Jesus said we are to love people who don't agree with us, don't share our values, who don't even like us. Love requires that we get involved in the messy situations of people's lives.

Jesus was frequently in trouble with religious leaders who were more concerned with their own reputations than helping those they were suppose to look out for. The religious leaders considered Jesus and his disciples unclean because of who they associated with, unclean sinners. Jesus was trying to rescue people from their destructive way of life. (Luke 5: 30-31, NIV.} - that's incredible.

Lettie – There have been times when what I learned as a child was not enough. I learned to be trusting and forgiving at the same time. If I forgive, I thought, will people use me and abuse me? Mother had taught me, "never let someone else use you." That was when I was small, younger. that's incredible.

Lettie – I have discerned that through reading Ana Holub, *Forgive and be Free,* "that forgiveness is a workout for the soul to make you stronger and more loving and compassionate at the same time. – that's incredible.

Lettie – Mother used to quote Mahatma Gandhi as did Holub: "The weak can never forgive. Forgiveness is an attribute of the strong."(Gandhi} p. 1. – that's incredible.

Lettie – "All forgiveness is self-forgiveness." We are responsible for all of our own mistakes in life, and "correcting our mistakes becomes essential to our peace of mind." P. 168. - that's incredible.

Lettie – Mother loved to travel and take us to visit our relatives and see other historical sites. We traveled all over the east coast because that is where our relatives lived. We went weekly to see Grandmom Sadie and Grandpop Herbert. They lived only a few miles away from us.

Many times Grandmom Sadie and Grandpop Herbert kept Daniel and Joseph at their house all day while Mother was working in her grocery store. We went to get my two younger brothers at night and bring them home. – that's incredible.

Lettie – Mother would say, "Who ever puts the child to bed at night is called 'Mama' by the child. Mother wanted all of us to call her mama or mother. - that's incredible.

Lettie - We visited Grandmom Hattie in Virginia on special occasions: funerals, 4th of July, Grandmom Hattie's birthday. She was born on August 15, 1894. - that's incredible.

Lettie – going places enhances and enriches your mind. Mother wanted only the best for us and the other children around us. She and Daddy sponsored trips for the Sunday school children and the choirs at our AME church. We went to beaches, museums, statue of liberty, Washington monument, Lincoln monument and such. - that's incredible.

Lettie – Many days Mother was reading Dale Carnegie's book, *How to Win Fiends and Influence People*. *This is Mother's motivational book because it teaches how to get along with people. It gives a positive approach as to how to have better relationships with other people. – that's incredible.*

Lettie – Mother taught us that we live in a world of compromise. When we are facing difficulties and challenges, we have to negotiate to arrive at a solution or solve the problem.

Back to the Beginning

"Grandma, you got way off the story about the day you were born," said Victoria. "What happened after you came back to life.?"

Tracie, Victoria's mother, said," Victoria, Grandma is tired. She has been telling you stories ever since we got to her house. It's almost time to go."

Victoria said, "But I want to hear."

"OK, the day I was born, I was on the ceiling with my angel. I saw everything that happened that day. I don't think I could see or hear but I felt a "presence" and I knew what was going on around me, even things that were not in the little bedroom. Later I realized it was the Holy Spirit. God was preparing me for life. He wanted me to help my mother and father and all mankind."

"Grandma, when you were a kid, what did you do," asked Kiara.

"Well here goes another story that is not in a straight line as I promised you guys earlier."

CHAPTER V

MY CHILDHOOD JOBS

"Grandma, as a child, what did you have to do, I mean besides play?" asked Amelia Grai"

"I have to do a lot around the house, like clean down stairs, clean my room, all that kind of stuff. Sometime, I help at Grandmother Chase's restaurant. But I don't get paid," she said.

"Amelia Grai, I remember doing many types of different jobs as a child and young teenager. Working for someone else requires being humble and having a good work ethic," I said.

I continued, "when I was a real little girl, I helped my mother in her grocery store. That was my first job. Customers would come in to buy items, like Campbell soup and Mother would reach me up to the shelf to get it, until she got smart and put a small table under the counter and put can goods and other items like bread and bags of sugar on the table so I could reach it by myself. This was before I went to elementary school. I was about four or five.

Then when Nancy and Hattie were born, I also helped with them, holding them, feeding them and changing them. That was a lot of fun for me.

"I had two little sisters to pet and play with. I remember people telling me to put those children down, especially Hattie because she was so plump.

They would say, "that baby weighs more you do when I was carrying her on my left hip. She was a little fat butterball, just as pretty as she could be."

I helped Mother around the house inside and out. She always had two gardens, one on the side of the house and the other in the back of the house.

Before going to the grocery store each morning, Mother, would go out to her gardens and hoe and pick the vegetables. She carried me with her.

I learned to pick crops early in life because she taught me. By the time I was old enough to help Mother in the garden and in the grocery store, my two older siblings were attending elementary school.

Two younger brothers were born and Uncle Clarence and Grandpop Herbert would come to our house and get them. Daniel and Joseph stayed at Grandmom and Grandpop Harper's house many days until Daddy and Mother went to get them.

Grandmom Sadie often kept Daniel and Joseph at her house until they got old enough to help around our house. I stayed with Mother and helped her inside the house, in the garden and the grocery store. We always had fresh fruit and vegetables to eat and so did all the neighbors.

Some of the fresh produce was taken into the grocery store for sale or give away.

Mother had a slogan: "Work with your head, your heart and your hands." She was always singing in the garden and humming in the house and grocery store.

I strongly believe that God used Mother and me in many instances to help someone else who had a greater need than we did. As I look back over my young days and my whole life, I feel that God relied on us to touch the lives of others and be a blessing to them.

By the time I was school age I had two younger sisters – Nancy and Hattie. I felt blessed. I always did love my two younger sisters a lot. When I came home from school each day, Mother turned them over to me to see to their needs. I enjoyed those two little girls.

Hattie got mean and Nancy stayed calm and humble.

Amelia Grai said, "I know about that. I have three younger sisters."

Daddy began building a restaurant. The store was still intact. Every Friday and Saturday, Mother would cook big pots of greens, and make potato salad, fried chicken and chitlins to sell in the restaurant. She made oyster fritters and baked sweet potato pies for the restaurant.

Soldiers were coming home from the war, World War II. Daddy and Mother were feeding them. There were other persons in the neighborhood who could not care for themselves.

"Wow! Grandma, you all were awesome," said Christian-Paris. "You wanted to help the whole world."

I said, "Mother felt that when you are sensitive to the needs of other people and the promptings of the Holy Spirit and are willing to do the will of God, you will touch the lives of those around you in a positive and special way."

"Live your life to the fullest by helping someone along the way."

"Yes, many persons came to our store/restaurant and said they were coming to church on Sunday. Our store/restaurant was a magnet for the church. Mother always had an encouraging word or a comforting smile or touch for all those she came into contact with. There were immediate opportunities to pray for someone who needed prayer."

There was an invalid woman who was also blind. She had a severely handicap, retarded son. Mother sent fresh vegetables and fruit, a big pot of homemade soup and bags of bead and crackers to this family every week. The lady could not talk, but her smile said it all.

Mother would pack our little red wagon with the groceries and hot food and let two of us carried it to our invalid neighbor.

There were no food stamps or welfare or social security checks in those days.

However, there were ration coupons distributed to families to purchase food such as sugar and flour. These ration coupons were given out according to the size of the family.

We had a large family, seven children and two adults. So we received more coupons than many of our neighbors.

Mother gave her teacher friend, Mrs. Peterson, a few ration coupons in exchange for cartons of strawberries and seafood. Mrs. Peterson was my first and second grade teacher.

Sometimes she asked me to dust and wash her dishes for her. In addition to the strawberries and seafood, she would give me a quarter and take me with her to her mother's house in Chester, Pennsylvania with her.

Mrs. Peterson's husband was terribly ill with black lung disease and my older brother, George stayed at their home with Mrs. Peterson's husband.

It was just neighbors one-on-one helping where we could.

I'd see Mother pass a slice of pie to a male customer who said, "I'll pay you next week, Miss Lettie." There was no 'next week.'

This was a soldier who was living in one of Daddy's little home built huts with no money to pay rent or for pie or fresh vegetables. Mother would also offer him a meal and a bag of bread. She knew that he would have to swallow his pride the next week and beg for another slice of pie. He was just a human being in need.

I said, "Amelia Grai, this is where you get your giving spirit. I see that in you and it is wonderful."

"You told me as you were preparing for your first communion, you had a vision to help someone. It came to fruition. You started your birthday bake sale which worked very well."

When the neighbors saw that Mother would let us work outside the home, they started asking if we could work in their homes and pick crops. Mother let us work for other people, but she told us to always take a sibling with us.

I started babysitting around the age of twelve. I worked for Mrs. Mason for three years after school. Mrs. Mason had three children while I worked for her. I worked from three p.m. until six p.m. every evening after school. I did not like the type of work that I did but our family needed the money, such as it was.

"Grandma, how much was it," asked Nia. She gave a little smile.

"Thirty-five cents every day after school. I earned thirty-five cent every day after school. I had to give Mother twenty five cent of it.

Well, Mrs. Mason did give me a bowl of black berry dumplings when I finished working. I did not like dumplings but I was hungry. I went to Mrs. Mason's house right after school and did not have time to get a bite to eat.

Mrs. Mason had a large pail of dirty diapers with poop in them waiting for me every afternoon. Remember she had three children, one right after the other. And she was pregnant again. They were Mennonite people. I did not like Mrs. Mason but I did like Mr. Mason. George, my older brother, worked for him.

"OH, Grandma."

Mrs. Mason's mother came over every day. She seemed to be coming to inspect the house. I definitely did not like her. She told Mrs. Mason that I should not come into the living room, stay in the kitchen and clean.

Once and a while, Mrs. Mason wanted me to change one of the babies. I came into to the living room and had to go out with the baby.

Another job I did not like at Mrs. Mason's house was scrubbing the kitchen floor and emptying the slop jars. Every time I picked up one, I thought to myself, "I will not do these jobs for anyone else. I will not work like this when I'm grown."

I did not know much about actual slavery when I was young, but I realized later how slaves must have felt doing these types of menial jobs.

I wound up changing the baby on the kitchen table, otherwise I would have changed the child on the floor.

Mennonite families are members of an Evangelical Protestant Christian sect opposed to taking oaths, holding public office or serving in the armed forces. Named after Menno Simons, they were established in 1492. (Riverside Webster's II New College Dictionary, p. 684.)

Come rain or come shine, I had to walk home through the woods, by a herd of fenced-in cattle, and out on the highway to get home every night. In the wintertime, it was dark by five o'clock.

I would say, "Marian, look to the light, look to the light. I was afraid of the dark."

Invariably, I would find a light peeping through the trees or from someone's window after I got through the woods.

Working for others requires humility. I had to have had a lot of it, because I kept going until I found another job.

That same summer of working for Mrs. Mason, a young white man and his wife walked into our yard asking for Mother. He asked Mother if sixteen year old Phyllis could babysit for them. He had gotten a recommendation for one of the Heath girls who babysat for people.

Mother called Phyllis down stairs and asked her to babysit for them. Phyllis said "no". She had something else she planned to do that evening.

I asked Mother if I could go. She said "yes."

After the couple left, Mother told me to take one of the boys with me so I could have company walking home that night. Daniel went with me and Joe came later.

There were two babies, one a year and a half years old and the other one was two months old. The couple left at six o'clock to go dancing at a bar, they told me. They would be back by ten o'clock.

The twenty-seven year old, two hundred thirty pound man returned home without his wife. When he entered the house, he told me that his wife wanted to stay a little longer. He came home to check on things.

He apparently forgot that Daniel had walked in with me to the house. Joe was in the house too. Joe came a little later thinking that this white family would have food in the house to eat.

"Oh, Wee, Grandma. I smell trouble," said Christian-Paris.

"Yes, I almost got raped that night. My two angels were Daniel and Joe. Joe was asleep but woke up hearing me struggling. Joe came to the bedroom door and called my name twice. The man stopped wrestling with me and pushed me toward the door.

"The man told me that he didn't mean no harm, but he had heard that black girls liked for men to 'play' with them. Joe didn't see what had happened but he knew that I upset. The man told me to sit down at the kitchen table while he got my pay.

He said he had planned to pay me one dollar but instead gave me two dollars. He told me that he worked on the road job with Daddy up in upper Delaware. Daddy would kill him or make him quit his job if I told Daddy about the man' s 'misbehavior.'

Walking home with my brothers, I was praying silently vowing and pledging to never tell Daddy because if he had a fight or killed this white man, he would go to jail. He couldn't stand the jail.

He used to tell my brothers, "if you get yourself in jail, don't call me. I never raised no jailbirds."

I never went back to that man's house and I never told mother or Daddy about the incident.

Luckily I found another job. It was in a doctor's office. The doctor's wife was very kind and caring. I worked for them every Wednesday after school and Saturday morning until noon. I worked in the office dusting the large pill bottles and dusting around the house. They had a vacuum cleaner which was adequate.

That's all I had to do. Mrs. Noble paid me five dollars for the two days. I loved working for her. Sometimes she gave me creamed coffee and a bowl of spaghetti. I didn't like the creamed coffee.

Dr. and Mrs. Noble asked me what I wanted to do when I grew up.

I was thinking, "I'm almost grown up now, I'm working, aren't I."

Mrs. Noble was a nurse. I felt this was a noble cause, so I told them that I wanted to be a nurse.

"Grandma, did you really want to be a nurse, or were you just saying that," quipped Kiara.

"Yes, I did want to be a nurse from the time I was seven.

"Grandma, you knew what you wanted to do when you were seven.? asked Victoria.

"I'm nine and I don't quite know what I want to do when I grow up."

"Yes, I wanted to be a nurse because when I was seven, my Grandmom Sadie got real sick. She had a heat stroke at the Fountain homestead. After a few nights in the hospital, Mother brought Grandmom Sadie home to our house."

She stayed with us for two years. Sometimes she got better, then she went back into a sick spell again. The whole family took turns feeding her, turning her, changing her, and just caring for her.

Grandmom Sadie talked to me and whispered many things about the family. Her father was blind and had been a slave. She informed me that they had been involved with the underground railroad at the Fountain homestead.

Uncle Clarence was not aware that the family was caught up in or embroiled in helping slaves to become free. Grandmom Sadie imparted family secrets that had to be kept in tack for the safety of everyone involved. Uncle Clarence was a small child when many episodes of slavery were going on.

Grandmom Sadie explained to me that life in a little town was by no means safe. There were things that she did not know. That is why she left the homestead, to try and have a better life for her children, her husband and herself. Caring for people like my grandmother was what I wanted to do.

So when the doctor and his wife asked me what I wanted as a career, I said a nurse. In my senior year in high school, I went with a classmate to University of Pennsylvania hospital to register for nurse's training.

I was given a questionnaire about my health. Then I was given a written test. While I took the written test, a lady entered the little cubicle I was sitting in, and asked me to come with her. She took me in a large office, had me to sit down and explained to me that I had not passed the physical test or questionnaire. I had to be five feet, three inches tall, weigh one hundred ten pounds and not have any chronic illness. I did not meet that criteria. I was too short, didn't weigh enough and had a chronic illness – asthma.

I informed Dr. and Mrs. Noble of my interview. They became angry. This was their school and they wanted me to go there to break the color or racial barrier. Dr. Noble planned to write the school a letter concerning this issue.

I told them that I had applied to several colleges and planned to attend one of them and that he should not write the letter on my behalf.

I was accepted at the three colleges and planned to attend Delaware State College (Now University.) I remember when I was a freshman right after I got to Delaware State University, I was told that I had received a scholarship in music.

On my application which my music teacher in high school helped me fill out, I put as my major: music.

My music scholarship was announced during my first year in college at a choir festival. We sang and then my choir director announced that I had been recommended by my high school music teacher. Mr. John Williams had recommended that I receive this scholarship as I had helped him with the choir music for four years in high school. Naturally his influence got me the scholarship. He was my angel.

I started out in music for two years, then changed my major to psychology and sociology. I did not want to be a music teacher as my mother wanted me to be. I wanted to be a social worker. When I changed my major, my new advisor explained that I would have to get a masters degree in social work and then maybe I still could not get a job.

"Take history and continue in music," Dr. Thompson said.

"Well, I was hearing from Dr. Thompson the same thing that I was hearing from my mother. Instead of changing my mind about being a social worker, I was determined to do both.

I went home from college every chance I got to play for my little AME church. I always played for the children and Mother played for adults. I lost the scholarship in music and I never heard of anyone else receiving a music scholarship from Delaware State College while I was there. I surmised that my two music teachers, Mr. William from high school and Ms. Grant from the college got together and pooled resources to give me that scholarship. I blew it but I did what I had to do," I said.

"Grandma you defied your mother and your teacher," Kiara said.

"Yes I did. I was a stubborn little cuss, but remember God gave me my mission when I was an infant, a day old. And my angel stayed with me. The Fall of my junior year in college, I received an additional amount of money on my Delaware Scholarship which made up for not getting the music scholarship my last two years in school." I was also given a job with the president of the college.

I was privileged to travel with his family to Boston, New York and Virginia during school holidays. My love for traveling was enhanced. I saw the Boston Harbor, The Commons, Christopher Adocks grave, Prince Hall Mason memorial."

"I was not trying to be disobedient to my mother and teacher. And I had much worse situations than that where my angel had to pull me out."

"From the time I was little, I was saying 'Yea thou I walk through the valley of the shadow of death, I will fear no evil, for thou art with me.' (Ps.23:4 KJV).

The day I was born, I could not see, I could not hear, I could only feel. I felt the hands of two people, two grandmothers who were mid-wives. Then I felt my angel and Jesus enter the room. Entered my life. I breathed my first breath. I was placed on my mother's breast and her life was restored.

This little four pound piece of human flesh became a human being ready to face the world with my mother and my angel(s). Mother rubbed my back and kissed me. I cried. Mother told the two grandmothers, "This is Marian."

She named me right then and there, that moment after her friend, Marian Anderson.

I told Mother about seeing heaven and my angel when I was born. I was two years old when I told her. She was crying because she had lost two babies. She stopped crying. She had me. There were other children to come. We bonded that moment forever.

Jesus had been in the room with us. Richard Allen was in the room. Grandmom Hattie and Grandmom Sadie were in the room. It was a powerful time. My life work was determined. I just had to obey God. I remembered all of these things.

When I was nine years old, I was going into our AME church with Daddy and one of the Sunday school teachers. Daddy was the Sunday school superintendent at our church.

A new picture of Richard Allen was on the wall as we walked into the church.

"That's Richard Allen," I said.

"Yes, we just bought that picture so that you children would know who founded our AME church."

"But I've seen him before," I said.

"When? We just put the picture there," said Ms. Maggie Hammond. 'You could not have seen him before. I hung that picture yesterday."

This was the first time Daddy had heard me discuss Richard Allen.

"I saw him when I was a baby. I didn't know who he was." I said

"OK! Some more of your discombobulated stories, "said Ms. Hammond. "Didn't Rev Forman tell you not to bring that type of talk in here."

Daddy fell silent. I fell silent. He had begun believing me.

OH, well, I can show them better than I can tell them. I made up my mind not to tell people about my angel and Jesus. Just try and be good and show them what I had seen in heaven and had been instructed to do. I was going to independently do His will and not worry about what people thought.

Easier said than done. As a child, I constantly worried about what others thought of me. I was growing up fast.

Daddy told mother about the incident with Mrs. Hammond and the Richard Allen picture and that we both had become upset about it.

In the meantime, I started looking for information on Richard Allen. Besides finding out who Richard Allen was and when and where he was born which was February 14, 1760 in Philadelphia, he was noted as the first bishop of the African Methodist Episcopal church.

"Soon after Richard Allen was born to slave parents, his family was sold to a Delaware farmer. At age 17, he became a Methodist convert and at age 22, he was permitted to preach."

I continued my search for material on Allen. The more I found, the more I became interested.

According to the Encyclopedia Britannica, "Allen was ordained in 1784 at the first general conference of the Methodist Episcopal Church in Baltimore. "He was considered a talented candidate for the new denomination's ministry. In 1786, he bought his freedom and went to Philadelphia where he joined St. George Methodist Episcopal Church. Occasionally, he was permitted to preach to the congregation. He also conducted prayer services for the Negroes." P.278.

"Restrictions were placed on the number of Negroes who could attend. Dissatisfied with how the Negroes were treated (I heard one old minister say that Allen was kicked up from the alter as he was praying at the Methodist Episcopal Church), he left that church and organized an independent Methodist church."

"In 1787, Allen turned an old blacksmith shop into the first church for Negroes in the United States, His followers were known as Allenites.'

"In 1799, Allen became the first Negro to be officially ordained in the ministry of the Methodist Church. The organization of the Bethel Society led in1816 to the founding of the first African Methodist Episcopal church, which elected Richard Allen as its first Bishop." P. 279.

After the hupla at the Sunday school with Mrs. Hammond, Mother started talking to me about joining the church.

I though, "I already belonged to the church. I was only nine years old but I had attended that church all my life. It was one door from my house."

"You have to go on 'the mourner's bench' and seek Jesus Christ," Mother said.

"My nine year old brain was telling me that I didn't have to seek Christ. I had Christ already."

Kiara said, "Grandma, you were caught between a rock and a hard place"

"Kiara, where did you hear that saying."

"From my other grandfather Redmond.

Anyway, you have to do what your parents tell you, or you'll get into trouble. Mother admonished me to do what my two older siblings did. They went on the 'mourner's bench', got on their knees, let the old preacher man, Rev Rockwell put his hands on their head. He prayed and ranted and raved. Then he assigned them a class leader." They were members of the little AME church.

"Well, it was my turn. The day I got on the 'mourner's bench', my best friend, Geraldine went too. We were both nine years old. We put our heads down and tried not to listen to what the old preacher was saying. He was preaching 'hell and brimstone.' He simultaneously put one hand on my head and the other hand on Geraldine's head. He asked us some questions and we simultaneously said 'yes'.

I was thinking 'I know more about heaven than he does because he's just preaching about hell. He told us to rise and go back to our seats after he baptized us.

"Rev, Rockwell thought we were crying but we were laughing so hard, we cried," I said.

Big Mike said" Ma, no wonder you raised us like you did. You had a mission in mind. That's some powerful stuff you are telling these kids. You never spoke to us like that."

"But when someone can repeat their story twice, they're telling the truth," said Lil Mike.

"Grandma, you got a good memory and you're old now. I believe all these things happened to you because you could not have made that information up," Christian-Paris mused.

The children and adults laughed because Christian-Paris called me old and because I had laughed during my baptism. I had pleased my mother at nine years old. I didn't mind their laughing at me at all.

"Thank you, 'Cree Pete' my nick name of Christian –Paris. I couldn't have made these stories up if I tried. I have a deep infinity for working with children because they are more trusting."

I know now why Mother made me go on the mourner's bench. It was so I could get along with the church folk and be obedient and not sass the adults. Mother realized that I was strong willed and determined. She came to the realization that my neighbors and friends did not understand me. She did not want me to be a loner and isolate myself. Mother was the special person in my life and she was my friend.

"Christian-Paris and Lil Mike, I have a great memory now. But one time I lost my memory due to an accident. It was in New Orleans," I said.

Grandpa Bert's attention was peeked again. I can read his body language very well.

"I remember that we had an accident in New Orleans a long time ago and you had to go to the hospital because you had a whiplash. When I came into your hospital room, you were smiling."

I took your hand and you said "Hi."

"I know, but I didn't know who you were. I tried to figure out who you were because of what you said to me."

"What did I say to you?" asked Grandpa Bert.

Grandpa Bert said, "Its been so long ago, I had forgotten the accident. I was taking you back to work that Sunday night. You had to go to work on Monday morning at the Welfare department."

"Right," I said. "A car had stopped in front of us to turn and go back the other way on Gentilly street. We stopped behind him and another car hit us from behind. All I remembered for the two days that I was in the hospital was what your face looked like."

"You looked like someone I used to know. I didn't know your name and I didn't know my name. When I went back to work several days later, my supervisor sent me home because my neck was in a brace. I had never been in a serious accident before."

We as children had traveled so many times before to see relatives and Daddy had never had an accident. I knew to pray but that's all I knew at the time."

"We got the car fixed, my memory came back to me and we were OK. Other than that, I have never had a lapse in memory before or since, except in spelling. "

Laughter filled the room.

Karen, my daughter, said, "Mother, I never heard you tell that story before."

"I forgot it," I said.

More laughter.

As I said before, when we were children in elementary and high school, we were always taking trips in Delaware and out of state to see our relatives and friends. Mother had many friends in New Jersey and Maryland. We had relatives in Philadelphia and New York. We not only traveled socially but Mother played for churches and we sang.

She formed a Heath Quartette and had the four oldest children singing from the time we were three or four years old. I am so glad that Heath quartette did not stick. I would have hated that type of life. That just was not me even though I love to sing and have sung in choirs in church, elementary school, high school, college and now in church choirs.

Mother understood that we wanted other careers and let us go. During high school, Mother started telling me, "Marian, go away and make your own way. Don't stay here, there's nothing here for you."

That's when I decided to become a social worker.

She saw that boys were hanging around our house, some younger, some older. They did not want to finish high school but just stay around home. She wanted me to finish high school, go away to college and make something of myself. She also knew that I had a lot of influence on my other siblings and felt that I could entice them to go to college and follow a good career.

At that point, Mother's teachings brought pressure to bear on me. She induced me to try and get as far away from home and follow my heart. Well, social work it was, I decided. My first job was in New Orleans after completing my masters degree in psychological counseling at the New Orleans Baptist Seminary. I had completed one and a half years in the Atlanta University School of Social work and qualified to be a case worker.

Right after I started my career in social work, I had the accident which almost caused me to lose my beloved job. I prayed hard because I did not know what I was doing. Grandpa Bert stayed in New Orleans that week I had the accident and went with me on the bus as I went to work. He would meet me at the bus stop every evening. So I had not forgotten how and where to catch the bus.

Under Mother's influence, I went away to college at Delaware State University. Mother had attended the same college. She wanted me to go there. However she allowed me to select my own college, "saying you should be proud of the school that you put beside your name."

> It actually was my choice. It was a wonderful time for me. I was not far from home. At first I had planned to attend a college in Virginia or Washington, D.C. However, I received a music scholarship to attend Delaware State University and later a Delaware scholarship. This helped my family greatly. There were still four younger children at home in

Greenwood and they were all in school. My parents were struggling to keep me in college as well as supplying younger siblings with their needs.

By this time Mother was getting more sickly and staying at home more, only attending church to play for the choirs. She was a juvenile diabetic which meant she had been a diabetic all her life.

As often as I could, I came home to play for the children's choir. Once when Mother was critically ill, she asked me to play the piano for the children's choir and the adult choir at our church. I found out that she was hemorrhaging and having miscarriages. She was losing our siblings and she was getting weaker and more stressed out with her health issues.

During the fall semester of my senior year at Delaware State University, Mother was found on the floor in a coma when my two sisters, Nancy and Hattie, came home from high school. She was critically ill and was admitted to the hospital.

She had just had all her teeth pulled. I often wondered if that had something to do with her final stages of poor health.

She seemingly had a massive stroke, went into a coma for two months and was revived only the day before she died. She also had to have radiation treatment because she had somehow injured her leg and the sore would not heal.

I was traveling from college twice a week to see Mother on the bus or with Daddy or Uncle Clarence picking me up and our pastor of the AME church carrying me back to school. After the radiation, we saw slight signs of her movement and improvement.

On January 29, Mother sat up in her bed in the hospital and began singing. She sang, "God will take care of you" and "I will trust in the Lord 'till I die."

The nurses and a doctor came running. They thought a miracle had happened. It had.

Mother was saying "Good-bye." We were not there. I was not there. This was the only weekend in the two months of Mother's hospitalization that I had not gone to the hospital. It had snowed hard that weekend before and Uncle Clarence said that he could not come to get me.

Mother, however was at peace. She had not opened her eyes while she was in a coma. I think that at that moment Mother woke up, saw heaven, forgave herself, forgave everyone else and at that point she was free and ready to pass on.

"She opened her eyes," the nurses told us.

She had seen heaven. However, she did not recover. On January 30, 1961, Mother died.

"No wonder so many of us wait until we hit rock bottom and feel broken to find God and say yes to the changes he is making in our lives."

Helen Keller said" Death is no more than passing from one room into another. But there's a difference for me, you know. Because in that other room I shall be able to see."

"Grandma, I don't understand." Kiara who was listening intently was puzzled.

I replied, "Helen Keller was blind all her life."

NO career As A Missionary In Africa.

After Mother died, I was not only devastated about that, I had signed up to go on a tour of duty in Africa and work with Peace Core when I graduated from Delaware State University that spring. That wasn't to be.

My psychology advisor told me that I had just had a traumatic experience as I had just lost my mother. He felt that I should not go that far away from my family. He told me that a tour of duty in the Peace Core would destroy me and was out of the question. He did not sign my papers to go to Africa.

"I went on interviews to find a job my last semester in college. One interview I will never forget. It was a case worker position in a rural town in Pennsylvania whereby each case worker worked only with one mentally ill child at a time.

As a part of my interview, I was given a five year old boy to attend to that day. I was not mentally or physically up to that type of job at that time."

My next choice of a move was to go to Atlanta University School of Social Work. My mother had admonished me to not stay in Delaware. "Go away and make your own way," she said. I was trying to obey her. I felt that I was also trying to obey God, too.

"Attending Atlanta University is another whole story. Suffice it to say, I did attend for a year and a half." I transferred my credits to another school.

"Grandma, did you ever go to Africa?" said Victoria. "Hurry up and tell us because Daddy is getting ready to go."

"We have gone to Africa five times," I said.

In 1988 we went to Kenya with our tour group from Southern University.

We went to Togo on another trip with our tour group. That was a horrible trip. The facilities were so poor and we did not feel safe. We saw the raw essence of that country.

In 1990, we had a beautiful trip to Egypt for three weeks, or so it felt like three weeks. Our Southern University group had Dr. Raymond Lockett as our tour guide. He was so dynamic and high powered, we were all over overwhelmed. There were forty -six persons on that trip to Egypt. Many new people joined our tour group for that trip. After all, this was Egypt. We had a few conflicts. In the end of that trip, all was good.

Nancy and I went to Morocco, North Africa in 2015 with another tour group from the Baton Rouge area. That trip included an excursion of Portugal and Spain which was fabulous.

The most significant time that we spent to Africa was when your granddaddy Bert, aunt Nancy and I went to Senegal and Mali, West Africa in April, May and June, 2005. Five other ministers from the United Methodist Church were with us. Dr. Alonzo Campbell was our leader. Grandpa Bert was our senior pastor. We were the LAVIM group, LA Volunteers in Missions group.

We lived in Senegal in a spacious missionary home with a missionary family for several weeks. However, we spent most of our time with the children in the villages doing missionary work. We fed the children, read stories to them, assisted the doctors and nurses with dispensing medicine and sang music with the children. Our missionary leaders, Karen and Sebastian, whom we stayed with, found a keyboard for me to play. Sometimes we were out in the rural areas where there was no electricity.

Some of the boys played drums and taught us how to play drums. This was a good experience.

Each morning when we left the Karen and Sebastian Missionary house, we were met with small boys who were on the street begging. The family urged us not to feed or give money to the small boys.

"Why?" Several of our grandchildren asked at once.

"Because these little boys were working for a man who had bought them from their parents to raise money for his comfort and upkeep. If the children did not bring money to him, he did not feed them that day. He did not allow these boys to attend school. They were his slaves. They were only about four and five years old"

These young boys' begging for money on the street did not do them any good, only the man who had bought them. The man saw that we were from America and stood across the street each day to see if we were giving money to these small boys. He obviously figured we would give money to them since we were staying at the missionary house and apparently doing missionary work.

The missionary family requested that we not contribute to this madness.

We went on our way visiting in small villages and large townships. There were eight of us in the group. Dr. Alonzo Campbell was our leader and Rev. Bertrand Griffin, our senior pastor along with African tour guides helped us through many dangers and demanding situations in and near Senegal. It was hard grueling exhausting work but that was what we signed up for. I played and taught the music each day.

There were so many new sights to see, some beautiful and some heartbreaking. The children that we worked with were endearing and appreciative of what we were doing for them.

Sometimes I could not play the key board that was given to me by Karen (our missionary guide) to use. There was no electricity in the village. We played drums.

The boys taught us how to play drums. This was a most exciting and satisfying time in my life. I felt at home. I was at home. I felt these children's pain yet they were so happy to see us.

We went to Dakar and Goree Island and many other towns and villages. This is two of the places which peeked our interest about slavery. We had two tour guides, one was especially interesting on the Goree Island slave house tour and slave ship tour. This ship was one of the slave ships (or one like it) that had carried slaves to different parts of the world. Our ancestors came across the Atlantic Slave Trade ships and were a part of some of those ships centuries ago.

Our older special tour guide told us to call him Beloved John. He gave us a book about slavery, *The Slave House of Goree Island*, written by Boubacar Joseph Hdiave. The book was partially written in French so Beloved John had to read parts of it to us. He told us that slaves were used in their own country, Africa, way before they were taken to other continents and countries.

However, African life was deeply interrupted by European settlements into the African continent.

Factions such as increasing populations of missionaries, farmers, officials, traders and different races of people brought many changes to African life.

Beloved John was incensed as he talked to us. He felt that we should know how he felt about the ancient times as he knew them.

"Your group is the only black group of missionaries that I have ever seen to come from America to western Africa, to Senegal or Mali from America," he said.

"I am glad to see you. I love each of you. You have survived slavery in your own country. I have survived slavery in my country."

I could ascertain what he was saying. We as Africans were resilient, strong and courageous.

During the last two days of our missionary work in West Africa, we had good-bye parties at two of the villages where we fed nine hundred children one day and a thousand, five hundred children the next day from surrounding areas and villages. The adults and missionaries from different church groups ate in a large pavilion where it was shady and cool.

The children sat on the ground and ate from large troughs with their hands. They were given water to drink in small cups.

I was very incensed about this. We were not allowed to mingle with the children a few days before we left.

We paid for the parties for the children and we wanted to share with them, not just the adult African dignitaries who were visiting the U.S. missionaries from the United Methodist Church. When we spoke to our missionary leader about this incident, she said that there were too many children to have chairs and plates for them. We had to go with the flow.

Our last treat for the children was to give them bags of candy, cookies and bubble gum. The African dignitaries asked us to leave the treats with them and they would give them out to the children when they got back on buses or walked home.

We as the United States missionaries wanted moments with the African children to be memorable ones. We asked the children to gather around us so that we could teach them another song. After we sang, we gave the children their treats we had brought for them. Our missionary friends and tour guides helped us to pass out the treats. Some of the older children helped too.

Anyway, I learned this song while I was over there in Senegal and taught each of the groups we interacted with.

The children loved to sing and their parents loved to see them happy. This is one of the last songs that I taught them.

We Come From The Water

We come from the water, all of us the water. Go back to the water and turn the world around.

We come from the fire, all of us the fire. Go back to the fire and turn the world around.

We come from the spirit, all of us the Spirit. Go back to the Spirit and turn the world around.

OH, OH-OOO, Turn the world around. OH,OH-OOO turn the world around.

I tried to teach them what the song meant, all of us are a part of God's creation uniquely made by our creator. Everything belongs to God. We are in His world. We are all his children and we belong to Him. Love God and love one another.

I hoped the adults learned a lesson from us, also.

Jesus said, "let the children come to me."

A LIVING *GHOST*

"Grandma, you said that you keep seeing ghosts," said Kiara.

Victoria said, "I like ghost stories, Grandma. Keep going."

As I told you earlier, most people are afraid of ghosts because they come with the purpose of frightening people. My ghost must be my angels because they come to me to help me or to inform me of something. They must be a part of my angel network.

Well, this story is a little strange because this person is still living. I saw her before I knew her name. I was a counselor-at- large at Southern University. I had established two therapy groups. We had T-group sessions every Tuesdays and Thursdays in my office.

I worked mostly with freshmen students. I was conducting one of my T-groups on this particular Thursday afternoon. I saw a young woman peeping in my office window. When my therapy group was over, this young lady entered my office.

She came in and said, "Mrs. Griffin, Right?"

"Yes, I am Mrs. Griffin. What is your name?"

"My name is Jeanette."

"Where are you from, Jeanette."

"Opelousas," She said.

"I have seen you before, more than once," I told her.

"I've come by here several times but there is always someone in here, either an individual or your therapy group is in session. I have been praying that you would let me come in and talk to you."

"Why, Jeanette, you are always welcome to come in and talk. I am a licensed Professional Counselor. I am here for all students, especially freshmen students."

I could not tell Jeanette that I had seen her in my dreams twice. In fact, I don't think that I was actually asleep. She was taller than I am, larger in stature, fair complexioned.

I reiterated to my grandchildren, "One night I felt a 'presence'. I looked up and saw a young female hovering over me. It startled me. I jumped up and ran to my boys, Bertrand and Michael's room then to Karen's room. They were all sound asleep. I went back to my bedroom and stood watching my husband sleeping. I got back in the bed and tried to sleep but could not.

An old preacher's wife once told me, 'when you can't sleep at night, that means someone needs you to pray for them."

So I started praying, "Lord help the young woman in my sight. She needs something and I don't know what it is. Help her, Lord."

Jeanette was sitting there looking at me. Then out of the clear blue, she said, "Mrs. Griffin, can I go home with you and stay at your house for a little while?"

This shocked me. I had not had this type of request before. I did not anticipate this request. Students have requested a ride to the bus stop or to the down town bus station or store to buy something. But no one had made this request before. She seemed embarrassed at asking for help. She seemed to be putting aside whatever pride she had.

Then she said something even more preposterous. "I need a mother. My mother died when I was a baby."

"Wow," said Christian-Paris. "That was some bold. Jeanette did not know you or anything about you."

"Christian-Paris, apparently she felt a connection with me and felt that I could help her even though we had not talked."

I began to realize that this young lady was still grieving or had just really begun to grieve.

According to Edelman, "Grief doesn't vanish because we try to lock it up in a sealed drawer, yet that's the way many of us are encouraged to cope: ignore the pain, and it'll go away." {P. 11.}

Evelyn Williams, a Case Social Worker and a therapist who led bereavement groups for collage age students at Duke University believed that we know when the moment to grieve or mourn arrives.

She saw students who had loss parents in their childhood. They found their way into groups in college, prepared to discuss their losses for the first time. Once they had physically separated themselves from their families and achieved the psychological and emotional stability they needed to mourn without the fear of abandonment or collapse, they could face their grief head-on. Our psyches seem to support us until we're able to confront the pain, and then the internal alarm clock rings, telling us it's time to wake up and go to work." p. 12.

"Experiencing that intense emotion is what helps us, ultimately, to accept that our mothers are done." p. 12

I was looking at the young person that I had seen not in a dream but as I was awakening. When I actually saw her, she was much taller than I am and the side of her face was turned toward me. I knew she was not one of my three children because they were small elementary children. She was either very fair complexioned or she was a ghost. I thought the latter was the case.

Every statement Jeanette made inspired and encouraged me to help her. In this multi-faceted fast-paced world, it is easy to forget that we are a part of a community and all need help.

Many families are in crisis, especially college students who are away from home. Some students come with financial, psychological, sociological and physical problems. I know this stressful time because I have been involved in it myself. I have had to ask for help myself and it was not easy.

I wanted Jeanette to know what she was asking me to do for her.

"Jeanette, I have three small children at home. They are nine years old, six years old and five years old. I do not know if you can put up with small children."

Jeanette answered, "Mrs. Griffin, I love small children. I'll even baby sit for you."

Without calling up my husband Bert about the situation, as he was probably not at home from work yet, I told Jeanette to go get an overnight bag and come right on back. I had to pick up my kids from school.

"OH, Grandma," said Amelia-Grai. "You didn't tell Grandpa first. What did Grandpa say?"

"Well as you know," I said, "Grandpa Bert is a minister. In fact, he is a chaplain and is constantly involved with clients who are in crisis."

Compassion is our business. That is why my husband and I do everything we can to serve people and our community.

Besides, Grandpa Bert trusted my judgment. He knew I could and would make wise decisions. But at the moment, I was more concerned about the young lady before me. Somehow someone was asking me to help her. I had to yield to the task at hand."

"Grandma, what was wrong with Jeanette? said Kiara. I'm hurting for her already and I don't know what was the matter with her."

"Children, in our own lives we cannot alternately deal with things as they happen. Most people start with disadvantages and obstacles and somehow work with whatever gains are possible for them," I said.

"Focus on the moment, not the monsters that may or may not be ahead." Holiday, p.47.

"Jeanette was grieving for her deceased mother and an ill, then deceased grandmother. That first night that Jeanette spent with us, Jeanette and I talked. She related that her mother had been killed when she was a month old.," I said.

I listened intently trying not to ask questions so that her conversation could flow. I cannot tell you all of the details because you are small children. Jeanette's father was the cause of her mother's death. He was in jail for life. Jeanette's mother lived for five days after the accident, then she died.

"I have never known a real mother," Jeanette said. "My grandmother was sick the whole time I was growing up. She had a heart condition and laid in the bed most of the time."

"My aunt Mary helped to raise me but she lived out of town. My aunts felt that I was a burden on my grandmother. We could never talk about my mother and father around my grandmother. She could not get over my mother's death and grieved until the end."

Little Olivia said "can ghosts be alive and still be dead,"

"Olivia, ghosts are believed to be dead people who come back to haunt living people," I said. (*Webster's II New College Dictionary, p.470*).

"When I saw a young *person* as I was half awake before I met Jeanette, I may have been seeing the ghost of her mother."

"I can't really answer your question, Olivia. Ghosts are a mystery and only God knows what they are all about."

"I do not know why they visit living people. There may be many different reasons."

Sophia apparently was listening. She was on the sofa with Grandpa Bert. She put her feet on his lap and said, "You're a ghost, Grandpa, You're a ghost."

Tracie, Sophia's mother, told Sophia to take her feet off of Grandpa and sit up. "Stop and come over here to me, Sophia."

I continued," Jeanette was only a freshman in college but she had come with many problems. She was struggling with her classes, she could not get along with her roommate and she had a strenuous burden to carry. Grief and guilt."

"I understood somewhat her efforts to survive all the frustrations and desperation that she had to bare because I lost my mother when I was in college but I had known my mother and had been raised by her and my father. I had a mother, a very good one at that. Jeanette did not have a mother to raise and nurture her."

Nia said, "Grandma, I feel sorry for Jeanette even though I don't know her."

"Yes," I said. She had her problems. There were severe obstacles in her past; a deceased mother, a father in jail, a sick grandmother and aunts who hardly knew her."

Well, Jeanette stayed with us many nights especially in the summertime. She was a good cook and helped around the house and stayed in college. She made a great gumbo. I could see the healing taking place. She became my children's big sister, especially Karen.

Karen had always wanted a sister, as she told me, "my brother has a brother. I want a sister." Well we did not have a sister for her. So she invented a family of sisters. She had Mary and Tabathia in elementary school. In high school and college she had Denise and Michelle. As an adult, as in now, she has Sanettria and Chanta. All of these friends were real live sisters to Karen. But Jeanette had become her big sister for life.

I pondered something I read a few days ago as I heard our pastor, Rev Hills say, "my brothers and my sisters."

He says it often and I have been passing it off as just a phrase that pastors use. Follmi states in his book, Origins that "the family in Africa is always extended."

In Africa, "You would not refer to your cousins as 'cousins because that would be an insult. So your cousins are your sisters and brothers. Your nieces and nephews are your children. Your aunts and uncles are your mothes and fathers. Children are also encouraged to call other persons outside the family mothers and fathers, sisters and brothers." Africa oral tradition, Follmi.

Karen was absolutely right. Her best friends are her sisters.

Now I know why we call church members 'sisters and brothers'.

I also realize why black men walk up to each other and say, "What's happening, bro or What's up my brother."

Jeanette moved in with us. She changed her faith or religion from catholic to full gospel Baptist. She had me take her on the Southern University campus at five o'clock many mornings to pray with a group of students. They interacted with *Up With People, a group of students who had formed a singing choir that went from college campus to college campus to sing gospel music.*

Holiday stated, "Our perceptions determine to an incredibly large degree what we are and are not capable of. In many ways they determine reality itself. When we believe in the obstacle itself more than in the goal, which will inevitably triumph? Though of course we don't control reality itself, our perceptions do influence it. (p. 51.)

Jeanette grew up and moved to Houston with an elderly uncle and finished college there. We became her family up until today. Her uncle died and we went to the funeral. Jeanette's older brother died. We went to that funeral. Jeanette calls us regularly and stops by to see us and stays with us whenever she is in Louisiana. We have gone to her family weddings and baby christening. I have accepted the fact that I am Jeanette's 'proxy' mother.

Amelia's Vision

Amelia began telling us about her 'presence' experience or a vision. She had a vision one day as she prepared for her first communion. She came to her mother and father and stated that she had so much and she had good things in her life that she did not want any more birthday parties. She wanted to raise money to help others. Whatever she got for her birthday, she wanted to give it to charity. Thus her idea was to have a bake sale and give all the proceeds to charity. "I felt God was telling me to give something to others in poverty."

Kiara said, "Amelia, do you know what poverty is?"

"Yes", said Amelia. "First I want to help my mother and father because they want us to be well fed, well clothed and do good in school. We do not always do right."

"Remember I told you that, Grandma? That sometimes we eat up all the food and Dad has to come home from work and go back to the grocery store and buy some more food because we ate it all up. I want to help my parents. I know I have good parents."

"Then I want to help others," she said.

"Some of my friends at school do not have as much as I have, I want to help. I decided to have a bake sale for my birthday and give all the money to charity," said Amelia Grai.

Amelia Grai did have a bake sale for her birthday each January 18. She gives the proceeds to the Daughters of Charity Health clinics where it was much needed. Each year she raises approximately one thousand dollars in one day at her home in New Orleans.

Amelia Grai and her mother, Tracie, bake cakes and cup cakes for days to be used for the bake cake. Her friends, family and the neighbors attend Amelia Grai's bake sale party and help her. We come every year from Baton Rouge and enjoy ourselves.

It is a great birthday party on January 18.

An another exceptionally happy time I had was at a music recital. Amelia Grai, along with her younger sister, Victoria are taking music lessons at the Music Center in New Orleans. We recently were invited to their music recital. Thinking that each grandchild was going to play the piano, we were prepared to hear them play a solo on the piano, as grandpa Bert and I had heard them do at their home.

Suffice it to say, "we were thoroughly surprised to see Amelia Grai and Victoria's names on the program as being a member of the Intermediate Strings Group. I was thrilled.

"I had no idea that you both were playing two instruments -both the piano and violin," I told them.

"My mother had always wanted us to play one or two instruments. We wanted our children to play one or two instruments. Now our grandchildren are playing two instruments. We have come full circle."

Lil Mike is playing a saxophone and piano. Christian– Paris is playing the piano and violin. Nia and Kiara took piano as small children.

"Olivia and Sophia, what instruments will you play?"

When Big Mike, his wife Tracie and their five child children prepared to leave to return to New Orleans, we went outside to bid them good-bye.

The older grandchildren, Nia, Kiara and Christian – Paris came back into the house. Bertrand II was getting ready to return home.

I realize that our conversation with the little ones made everyone vulnerable but we had valuable therapeutic and inspiring expressions. Different age groups have to adjust to each other. You two are young ladies and may not want to share some of your thoughts and mind boggling experiences with others.

Nia said tersely. "We didn't have enough time. Listening to the younger children was tremendously satisfying to me. Obviously some of the experiences that I have had as a teenager may have been inappropriate and I could not share them with little children."

Kiara said, "I agree with Nia. I would be able to share my thoughts with people my own age. I enjoyed it though. It was all good."

"You took the words right out of my mouth. I'll say 'amen' to that," repeated Christian-Paris.

It was so exultingly marked with great joy. Your diary and our great grandmother were awesome.

CHAPTER VI

MY SACRED SPACE

This diary is just words. The meaning behind these words is God. God is everything; everything belongs to him. Nothing exists without the infusion of the Holy Spirit.

"Grandma," said Kiara, "you are awesome. You are getting more and more philosophical. I understand some of what you are saying but I'm a long ways from comprehending or recognizing what you mean."

"First, Kiara, only God is actually awesome."

You have heard the song: "You're an awesome God."

"We as human beings are also spiritual but we are no where near Jesus who is God in person."

"The younger five grandchildren have gone home to New Orleans. I must say that we shared much knowledge and insight with each other. I have prayerfully allowed you into my 'sacred space.'

Ana Holub, in her book, Forgive and Be Free, states that, "sacred space is not a place. Sacred space doesn't have walls or a floor, and it definitely doesn't have a roof or ceiling. What she was describing was "more like a sacred float into a state of consciousness-the river's divine return to the primordial sea." p. 67.

My diary reveals spiritual support and growth for all. We cannot put this knowledge back in the box," I mused.

Holub states "I need to continue with my inner momentary self, trusting that everything was unfolding perfectly. Feeling so much joy and openness in my body (and mind), I gave myself freedom simply to enjoy the sensation and the freedom that come from releasing old memories out of my body, heart and mind." p. 63.

Christian-Paris stated, "I am almost getting it but maybe I'm too young to know what you are talking about."

"Christian -Paris, I started off by saying, I want you to know that I am a spiritual being. I am and you are an empty vessel put on this earth to complete a mission from God.

I have an angel or many angels through the years to guide me. They are sent from God.

Holub, once again states that "what our spiritual awakening looks like on the outside doesn't matter, our shift of consciousness may be flamboyantly or extremely subtle. Most likely they fall somewhere in between." p. 64.

Except in a few rare cases, awakening happens within us in thousands of baby steps. Some are obvious and life-changing but many others are often mysterious and not even available to our conscious mind." p. 139.

"My story is only a symbol," I said.

My primary goal is to give you a peek at the past or the preserving of the past only to enhance your knowledge for the future. I am focusing on my family only because it's the one I know.

One of the TV commentators from Farmer's Insurance states, "I know a thing or to, cause I've seen a thing or two."

Let me proceed to tell you where we came from. I was born in a little cabin(shack) on a white man's large farm in Delaware, in the deep south it would have been called a plantation.

My mother was an educated woman born in Philadelphia on December 6, 1908. She attended elementary school for five years in Philly. On to Delaware in junior high school for two years. Then she attended boarding school for four years in North Carolina. Mother did not stop there.

She attended and graduated from Cheyney State University in classical music at Cheyney, Pennsylvania. Then to Delaware State University, where she graduated in elementary education.

Mother fell in love and married our father who was a brilliant man. He was the fifth great grandson of Nyo Khoban from Mali, West Africa, born in 1826 who walked out of her village due to no fault of her own. She came to America with her mother, Ana Khoban who was born in Mali, West Africa.

After reaching the colony of Virginia, Nyo was renamed Anna Lisa Coleman by her slave master. She was allowed to marry Steven Wise. Two of the Wise granddaughters married into the Heath family who came from Ghana, West Africa into the British West Indies, later to be sold to a Plantation owner in the Commonwealth of Virginia.

These are very minute details of our ancestral background factually proven by DNA and Ancestry.com, United States Federal Census Reports, Family Bibles, birth certificates, death Certificates, marriage certificates and military draft reports. I am proud of my background.

Someone said, "don't look back, look forward."

"I say look back just to know your roots. You have deep roots," I said.

"By roots, I want you to pay attention to this description of the sequoi tree," I said.

"This tree is among the world's largest and most enduring organisms. It can grow to 300 feet in height, weigh over 2.5 million pounds and live for 3,000 years. The majestic sequoia tree owes much of its size and longevity to what lies below the surface: a twelve to fourteen feet deep matting of roots, spreading over as much as an acre of earth which firmly grounds its towering height and astonishing weight." (Mart Dehaan, author for Our Daily Bread. July, August, September, 2017.

I hope that this diary someday will give hope and optimism to future generations. We look at what happened to us, to our lives, but our mission is to focus on the future.

What is truly inspiring to me is our new generation, especially black children who will govern the world. They will.

When I look at you, our grandchildren, I realize that freedom is once again on the horizon. I'm giving all of you something to go home and ponder, to think about.

Looking back over my life, I know I am an ambassador for Christ. Just hold on. God will give each one of us opportunities and victories. Always remember God is the architect of your life. With God's help, you will succeed.

CONCLUSION

What a jewel my mother was. Writing this diary, which I have been writing all my life, has helped me to finally heal from loosing her after over fifty years.

I can stop crying each year around the anniversary of her death. But I can still cry if I want. She is still my mother.

I am writing this diary on behalf of my mother, Lettie for my siblings: living - George, Nancy and Joseph, deceased – Phyllis, Daniel and Hattie, in honor of Mother, my father, George Wesley Heath, Sr. our ancestors and in gratitude for our descendants - our children, our grandchildren and others to come.

This book is in honor of our ancestor and in gratitude for our descendants. The magnitude of writing this diary had impacted my life significantly. Our Lettie will live in our hearts forever.

BIBLIOGRAPHY

Anderson, Joan *Wester. Guardian Angels.* Chicago: Loyola Press, 2006.

Angelou, Maya. *The Heart of A Woman. New YorK: Random House, 1982.*

Aristide, Jean-Bertrand. *Eyes of The Heart.* Monroe, Me. Common Courage Press, 2000.

Arnold, Stephanie. *7 Seconds Dying Revealed Heaven. New York: HarperCollins, 2015.*

Barboza, Steven, ed. The African American Book of Values.

Briskin, Jacqueline. The Naked Heart. New York: Bantan Doubleday Bell Publishing Group, 1989.

Burpo, Todd. *Heaven is for Real.* Nashville, Tenn. Thomas Nelson, Inc. 2010.

Carter-Scott, Cherie. *If Success Is a Game, These Are The Rules.* New York: Broadway Books, 2000.

Carnegie, Dale. *How to Win Friends and Influence People. New York: Simon & Schuster Co. 1984.*

Cohn, Michael and Michael K. H. Platzer. *Black Men of The Sea. New York: Dodd, Mead and C Company, 1978.*

Collins, Randall. *Sociology of Marriage and Family.* Chicago: Nelson-Hall Company, 1940.

Cuddy, Amy. *Presence.* New York: Little, Brown and Company, 2015.

Dyer, Wayne W. *Real Magic Creating Miracles in Everyday Life.* New York: HarperCollins Pub. 1992:

Dungy, Tony. *Quiet Strength.* Illinois, Tyndale House Publishers, 2007.

Edelman Hope. *Motherless Daughters. New York: Bantam Doubleday Dell Publishing Group 1984.*

Fernandes, Sujatha. *Close to the Edge. New York: Verso Books, 2011.*

Fitzgerald, Helen. *The Mourning Handbook*. New York: Simon & Schuster, Inc., 1994.

Follmi, Dnielle and Oliver. *Origins African Wisdom for Every Day Harry N. Abrams, Inc, Publisher.*

Glassner, Barry and Rosanna Hertz. *Our Studies, Ourselves.* New York

Holmes, Marjorie. *I've Got to Talk to Somebody, God. New York: Doubleday, 1969.*

Holiday, Ryan. *The Obstacle Is The Way. New York: Penquin Group, 2014.*

Holub, Ana. *Forgive and Be Free. Woodbury, Mn. : Llewellyn Publications, 2014.*

Hughes, Langston. *The Negro Mother, The Collected Poems of Langston Hughes. Arnold Rampersad, ed. New York: Vintage Classics,1994.*

Lacy, Leslie. *Native Daughters.* New York: McMillion Publishing Company, Inc. 1974.

Lavalle, Victor. *Ecstatic. New York: Crown Publishing Co. 2002.*

Lesser, Elizabeth. *Broken Open. How Difficult Time can Help Us Grow.New York: Villard Book, 20004.*

Long, Jeffrey, MD. *Evidence of the African Life.*

Liversay, Howald. *Delaware Negroes,* 1865-1915 Delaware History 13, 1968.

Malik, Kenani, *Strange Fruit: Why Both Sides were Wrong in The Race Debate.* Oxford, England: One World, 2008.

McKnight, Reginald. *He Sleeps.* New York: Henry Holt and Company, 2001.

Meredith, James and William Doyle. *A Mission For God.* Africa Books Press, 2012.

Meyer, Joyce. *Living Beyond Your Feelings. New York: Hachette Book Group, 2011.*

Murphy, Laura. *Survivors of Slavery. New York: Columbia University Press,2014.*

Neal, Mary C.,MD. *7 Lessons from Heaven.* New York: Congergert Co., 2017.

Norris, Leslie P. *God's Early Morning Intervention,* Bloomington, In:. Xlibris, 2016.

Oliver, Stephanie Stokes. *Seven Soulful Secrets.* New York: Random House Pub. 2001.

Park, Manago. *Travel in the Interior of Africa* Describes Travels from Gambia through Senegal and Mali in the years 1695-1797.

Ramning, Cyndy. *All Mothers Work.* New York: Avon Books, 1996.

Rabey, Lois Moyday. *Women of Generous Spirit. Colorado Springs, Co.: Waterbrook Press, 1998.*

Rieger, Shay. *Our Family. New York: Lathroe,Lee and Sheoard Co. 1972.*

Roberts, Alison. *Wishing For A Miracle. Great Britain: Harlequin Mills & Boon Limited, 2010.*

Steel, Danielle. *Against All Odds. New York: Random House, 2017*

-------------------. *Precious Gifts. New York: Randon House, 2015.*

Sowell, Thomas. *The Vision of the Anointed. New York: HarperCollins Publishing Co., 1995.*

Still, William. *Underground Railroad Records.* Philadelphia, William Still Book Publishing Co, 1872.

Storr, Anthony, *Solitude A Return to the Self. New York: Free Press, 1988.*

Taylor, Kristin Clark. *Black Mother. New York: Doubleday, 2000.*

Walsh, Dan and Gary Smalley. *The Promise. New York: Thorndike Press, Published in 2014: 2014 Revell Books.*

Yamauchi, Edwin. *Africa and The Bible.* Ballo Book House Co. 2004.

Zook, Kristal. *Black Women's Lives.* New York: Nation Books, 2006

REFERENCE BOOKS

Laird, Charlton. Webster's New Roget's A-Z Thesaurus. Cleveland, Ohio: Wilet publishing co. 2003.

Riverside Webster's II New College Dictionary. New York: Houghton Mifflin Company, 1995.

The Holy Bible. New International Version. Michigan: Vondervan, 1973.

The New Encyclopedia Britannica, Volume 1. Chicago: Encyclopedia Britannica, Inc. First edition, 1768-1771, fifteen edition, 1986.

Sadie Mae Fountain Harper, born around 1888 in Delaware
, married August 6, 1904 and died January 15, 1949.

Marian Heath Griffin and Bertrand Griffin, Sr.'s 50th wedding anniversary
on March 23, 2013 surrounded by generational family members.

George Heath, Sr. and Lettie Harper Heath at a
Masonic Cotillion Ball in Maryland.

Hattie Drucilla Wise Heath, born in Accomack County,
Virginia on August 15, 1894, died on October 20, 1962.

Daniel Louis Heath, Sr. born November 21, 1940 in Delaware. He died on May 3, 2009 in Louisiana. Picture of his family taken after memorial service at St Mark United Methodist Church in Baton Rouge Louisiana.

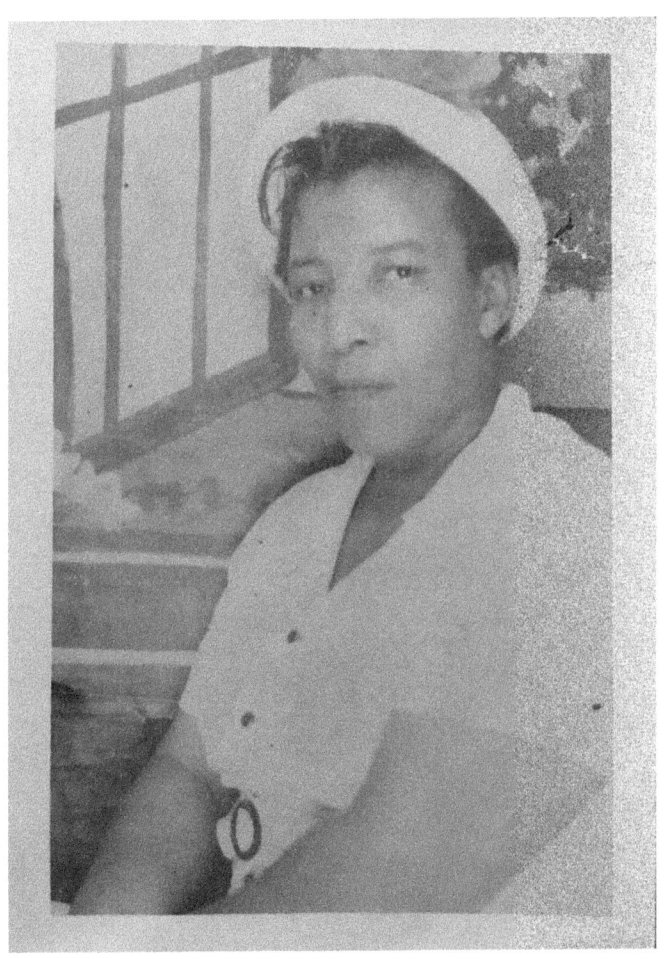

Lettie Sidney Harper Heath, born on December 6, 1908,
Married on April 1933 and died January 30, 1961.

CPSIA information can be obtained
at www.ICGtesting.com
Printed in the USA
BVHW03*1352170918
527708BV00005B/82/P

9 781984 548603